Be Happy

Encounters with Sadhguru Sri Sharavana Baba

CRAIG HAMILTON-PARKER

GOD IS EVERYWHERE
Copyright © 2018 Craig Hamilton-Parker

BE HAPPY
Copyright © 2021 Craig Hamilton-Parker

Author's website:
www.psychics.co.uk

Author's YouTube Channel:
https://www.youtube.com/user/psychicmovies

Sharavana Baba Websites:
http://omsharavanabhavamatham.org/
http://omsharavanabhavamatham.org.uk/

All rights reserved.

ISBN: 9798752357428

GOD IS EVERYWHERE

In part one of this book, first published as *God is Everywhere,* psychic mediums Craig & Jane Hamilton-Parker received a frightening message from the Agastya Naadi Sastra. It set them on an adventure to find a holy man who could help them change the course of destiny.

Through his contacts in India, Craig found a genuine Naadi that has the power to foresee future events with 100% accuracy. The oracle identified Sharavana Baba as the holy man who could turn the tide of providence and who could save their grandson's life. In a dash to meet the oracle's deadline, Craig and his wife Jane meet Sharavana Baba.

BE HAPPY

The book's second part, *Be Happy,* was written during the Covid 19 pandemic when the world felt far from happy and everyone worried for the future.

Craig sets off to India to spend time with Sharavana Baba during Maha Shivaratri. He discusses the world's future, what is happiness, and how can we find it in these troubled times.

Om Sharavana Bhava

CONTENTS

	Acknowledgments	I
1	The Naadi Predicts	Pg 1
2	First Meetings (Extract from Messages from the Universe)	Pg 7
3	Mystic Journey	Pg 19
4	The Shock Sinks in	Pg 25
5	The Naadi Remedies	Pg 29
6	Seeking a Holy Man	Pg 37
7	The London Ashram	Pg 43
8	Cosmic Trance	Pg 49
9	Barcelona	Pg 55
10	The Naga/Sarpa Loka	Pg 62
11	Who is Sharavana Baba?	Pg 70
12	The Sathya Sai Link	Pg 79
13	Coming Home	Pg 84
14	Rameshwaram	Pg 97
15	India Calls	Pg 104

16	Predictions	Pg 113
17	To India	Pg 142
18	Indian Ashram	Pg 168
19	Meeting and Darshan	Pg 196
20	Strange Stories and Holy Fires	Pg 210
21	Ancient Oracles	Pg 240
22	Pandemic and Predictions	Pg 257
23	Remain Happy	Pg 269
	DISCOURSES	Pg 284

Acknowledgments

Thanks to:

Kim Paisol—Jiva Naadi research.
P. Gnanaprakasam (Mr Prakash)—Naadi Remedies.
Vivek Chhibba—Naadi research.
Alison and Ash – Making everything possible
Martin Pickering—book editing
Visnezh— Mandala Graphic—Freepik.com
Alison Parmar-Howse—research suggestions.
Professor Ramnath Narayanswamy—Naga research suggestions.
Om Sharavanabhava Trust - Checking factual content.

CHAPTER 1

The Naadi Predicts

My wife Jane and I are both mediums. We've spent most of our lives communicating with the dead and relaying timely messages of hope from the other side. Our main work is to give proof of life after death, but we also sometimes use our clairvoyance to guide people or to make prophecies about the future. As you can imagine, it's very unusual for both people in a marriage to be mediums.

About our Psychic Work

On the surface, we are just like any other family, except we are psychic. We have had our own TV shows, have done a controversial séance to communicate with the spirit of Princess Diana and more recently been in the press because many of my 2015 world predictions came true—including Donald

Trump's becoming president, the terrorist attacks in Nice and Britain leaving Europe.

We have worked a lot in the media, but most of our fees have been given to charity or put into our Foundation. This organization has a spiritual remit to build our own centre and does a lot of charitable work, including giving away cows, feeding beggars and helping an Indian school for the mentally subnormal.

The central message in many of my books and YouTube videos is that the world is now moving into better times and away from the shadows of the dark age called Kali Yuga. In the coming times, individuals—and eventually society at large—will awaken to the dawning light of spirituality. There will be a golden age when many holy men and women will walk the earth again.

Jane and I have given a great deal of time, and spiritual work to Spiritualism and have done many demonstrations of mediumship in the British Spiritualist Churches. In parallel to this, I have always had a deep interest in eastern spirituality and esoteric teachings. This philosophy has been with me since the age of 14, when I began learning yoga and meditation. (I'm now 67.) Jane and I have also been inspired by Sathya Sai Baba, whom we went to see in Puttaparthi, Andhra Pradesh, India in 1998.

The Naadi Sashtras

In my book *Messages from the Universe,* I explain how my world was turned upside down when I consulted the Naadi Sashtras from India. These are claimed to be over 5,000 years old and were written by the ancient sages of India. They contain the destiny of anyone who is able to find the true oracle and read words written on their palm-leaf pages. The Naadis told me my name, my parents' and siblings' names, my wife's name, my ex-wife's name and about all that has already happened to me and all that will happen to me in the future. It even gives the day I will die.

My friends Vivek Chhibba and Sri Saktibaanee (Kim Paisol) had independently sourced Naadi oracles that were genuine, and we were able to get a prediction for my future that could be verified by consulting unconnected oracles in different parts of India.

I came to understand that the great Indian sages of the past had conquered time. What they were saying is 100% true. They wrote their insights in Sanskrit on pages made from palm leaves called the Naadi-Sashtra (A Sashtra is a work of sacred scripture. They are also known as the Naadi Granthas. Granthas are manuscripts divided into 16 chapters or Kandams.) The leaves were translated into ancient Tamil language—called Vatteluttu—and have been copied and rewritten every 500 years.

Naadi astrology says the past, present and future lives of all humans were foreseen by Hindu sages in ancient times. There are different schools of thought as to the author of these leaves. The consensus is that they were written by a Tamil saint called Agastya (Agathiyar), who is said to have had divine revelations. The Naadi leaves were initially stored in the premises of Tanjore Saraswati Mahal Library of Tamil Nadu. The British Raj showed interest in the Naadi leaves concerned with herbs and medicine and future prediction but left most of the leaves to their loyal people. Some leaves were destroyed, and the remaining were auctioned during British rule. These leaves were bought by the families of astrologers in the Vaitheeswaran Koil temple located in the Indian state of Tamil Nadu. Shiva is worshipped as Vaidyanathar or Vaitheeswaran, meaning the "God of healing", and it is believed that prayers to Vaitheeswaran can cure diseases.

The oracle lays the future bare. It predicts all the good and bad things that will happen. There is even a section that lists incurable illnesses that the person will have. It also gives remedies to fix the future and help us to eradicate the effects of negative karma. In fact, this is its true purpose: to find out what karmic effects are blocking our path to salvation. To clear the way it will offer us remedies. These consist mainly of mantras, pujas, and charitable acts that will twist fate in our favour if done at specific times. For some, the remedies will fix life problems, but the hidden agenda is that the remedies are there to point you towards enlightenment.

Be Warned

Most Naadi readers are frauds. Some have enticing websites that promise much but may leave you more frightened than enlightened. In India, Naadi readers pester wealthy foreigners outside airports and so on to have expensive readings. The word 'Naadi' also means 'to search', so it may take you many years to find a genuine Naadi reader. The hard-sell Naadi websites should be avoided. And even some that I have used in the past have now become greedy, and the power of the Naadi has left them. Because of this tendency to corruption, I can no longer recommend Naadi readers. I only now introduce people I know very well or who are working with me to do charitable work and service.

Despite the numerous frauds, a precious few readers, hidden away in the Indian villages and backstreets, remain the true custodians of the manuscripts. I was lucky enough to be introduced to some of these readers who were able to tell me mind-boggling things about my life.

My leaf was found by looking at my thumbprint, which is used to find the bundle of leaves and the specific leaf that relates to me. Without knowing anything about me, the Naadi readers were able to tell me my parents' names, my ex-wife's name, my wife's name, as well as my name and the exact time of my birth. They knew of all the essential things that had happened throughout my life and were able to predict my future up to the day I die and into future incarnations.

The Naadi leaves are so incomprehensibly accurate that it has taken me years to come to terms with what they have to say. I now see the world from a completely different perspective, not as something 'out there' but as a reflection of the evolution of the spirit. And just when I thought that things couldn't get weirder, Sri Saktibaanee told me about the very rare Jeeva Naadi. These leaves are blanks. There is nothing written on them until you ask a question, and then the words appear on the surface as if written in light.

The Jeeva Naadi is a miraculous form of communication with saints who have entered a different state of existence. Could it be that the great maharishis, who speak through the leaves, live simultaneously in the past and in the present? What happens is beyond our comprehension.

A person can consult the Jeeva Naadi to get guidance and remedies for their life problems. They ask a question, and the words appear as letters of light—sometimes in the person's language making the consultation. Although I have not seen this with my own eyes, I have received messages via the Jeeva Naadi by proxy, and they have proved to be very accurate.

My encounters with the Naadis, the Jeeva Naadis and the Bhrigu Samhita set me on a great spiritual adventure. I went to India to do the remedies prescribed to help me eradicate the harmful effects of my past life karma. I took a cameraman with me, and we produced a film called *Mystic Journey to India,* and I wrote a book of the same title. (You can watch *Mystic Journey to India* on Amazon Prime.)

In India, I did pujas, and fire rituals, visited a holy man who could sleep in a pit of fire and did charitable acts such as feeding an orphanage and giving cows to poor people. It was an incredible adventure to extraordinary places, and at times I felt that I was experiencing a real-life version of *Indiana Jones and the Temple of Doom.*

CHAPTER 2

First Meetings

Before I set off to India to do the Naadi remedies, I stumbled upon Sadhguru Sri Sharavana Baba. A text arrived out of the blue. It was from my friend Vivek who had helped me to find my first Naadi readings.

"Craig, a fantastic guru, is visiting the UK," said the message that popped up on my phone as I strolled along with a grey, windy beach in Hampshire. "I have a powerful gut feeling that he wants to talk to you. I don't know quite what it's all about, but it has something to do with our work together with the Naadi prophecies."

Vivek had recently had an interview with Sri Sadhguru Sharavana in Croydon on one of his rare visits to London. He was to have one more appearance at a private home just fifteen minutes drive from my home in Eastleigh. Vivek felt that the coincidence was just too significant to miss, and he would put me in touch with the homeowner, then threatened to text me twice a day thereafter to remind me to go. There was no way he was going to let me off the hook! "You sit before him, and he will tell you everything. Take Jane with you. Please, please go. Trust me. He's just like Sathya Sai."

Vivek had mentioned Sri Sadhguru Sharavana before during our many long chats on Facebook about Sathya Sai Baba and other miracle-makers from India. He had told me about this Indian man who could read minds as if he were reading a book. You didn't even have to ask him a question. He would just tell you what you needed to know. Some Sathya Sai devotees had been drawn to him, too, and some had seen him transfigure into Sathya Sai Baba.

The only problem now was to talk Jane out of Sunday lunch, shopping, and a movie and get her to go with me on another wild goose chase. There was some resistance because the last time I took Jane to visit a guru, we went to see one we both felt was far from spiritual. This 'guru' claimed to be the reincarnation of Yogananda, and who dressed and modelled himself on Sathya Sai Baba, despite—we heard later—having been the only person ever to have been thrown out of the ashram.

When we stood together before this man, we both looked in his eyes and saw an ordinary man—someone whom we did not like at all. "This guy's a fake," whispered Jane "he's pretending to be something he's not, and these mugs are lapping it up."

Talking later to some of his original devotees reaffirmed our doubts, and we could see why so many of his first devotees had deserted him. The one thing he did have going for him was that he not only had a beautiful singing voice, but he could turn traditional *bhajans* and mantras into wonderful, beautiful compositions.

Our encounter with this 'guru' really worried me until I dreamt of Sathya Sai Baba, who put me straight. (If you ever have a dream about Sathya Sai Baba, you will come to understand that dreams about him are real encounters.)

Many of the dreams I've had about Sathya Sai Baba have been hilarious, and this was another one of those. He appeared to me dressed as Elvis Presley and was doing a rather bad Elvis impersonation. Even in the dream, it was side-splittingly funny to see Baba in the full Elvis garb—bling and sunglasses, too. After a few "Uhhhuh, Babys" and a bit of wobbly singing, he said to me: "Why have an impersonator when you can have the real thing? Don't worry about your friends. I will look after them."

Soon after that, the fake 'guru' announced to the consternation of everyone but Jane and me that he was closing his organization. The money had dried up, and there were some dreadful rumours circulating about him.

So it was with this experience in mind, and with my own over-enthusiasm for all things spiritual, that I needed to sidetrack Jane from her Sunday outings. Just because we were followers of Sathya Sai Baba when he was alive did not mean we should rule out seeing other gurus. I've always believed in taking personal responsibility for one's life. We must have the courage to think for ourselves. You don't need to grovel at the feet of gurus and beg for a favour. However, if a person is secure in themselves, gurus can be a boon, for they can help us to progress. If we become aware of the light within ourselves, then we will see the same light shining back at us in holy men. My take on things is that all the gurus are the same. They are the one clear light of the divine that shines and expresses its diversity through multiple stained glass windows.

Sadhguru Sri Sharavana Baba was born on 11th October 1979 in Sreekrishnapuram in the Palakkad district of Kerala in South India. He is the eighth child in a family of nine children. His devotees tell us that he was born self-realized and fully aware of His divinity. His devotees call him 'Babaji', and he is regarded as the divine incarnation of Lord Subramanya. (Lord Subramanya is also called Kartikeya, Murugan, Skanda and Kumara. This is the Hindu god of war and the son of Parvati and Shiva, brother of Ganesha, and a god whose life story has many versions in Hinduism. (To keep things simple, I'll hereafter speak of 'Lord Murugan').

Sharavana Baba had a humble background and suffered a lot of cruelty in his early life. It is claimed that he has produced many miracles. He now has ashrams worldwide, and the emphasis of his teachings is love, faith, devotion, surrender, and selfless service. His organization does a lot of work feeding the poor and clothing the destitute through his trust called the 'Om Sharavana Baba Dharma Trust' set up in 2006.

Jane and I knew none of the above when we arrived at the house in Fareham, Hampshire. It was remarkable because this was not far from our home, and it was as if the guru had come directly to us.

We arrived a little too early. Jane's hopes for a shopping extravaganza had been dashed by now, and she fidgeted as we waited in the car. "I do hope this is not another one of your crazy, time-wasting 'days out' talking to some nutcase," she complained. "And you *have* told these people that we are coming? I feel a bit like a gate-crasher at a party." I reassured Jane that all would be fine.

When we entered, we were asked to take off our shoes and sit on the floor in the front room. Men on the right and women on the left. We were some of the first to arrive, but soon the room was filled with Indians. Everyone was very welcoming and excited at the prospect of the arrival of the guru.

The front room of the house had been transformed and looked like a temple of white and turquoise. A red silk carpet strewn with flowers ran through the middle of the room, leading to a golden chair at the front of the room where Sharavana Baba would sit. Visitors sat on both sides, and mantras and *bhajans* were sung to the accompaniment of a harmonium and drums. The Indians certainly know how to make a show when it comes to spiritual ceremonies and events—and all in an inconspicuous house, just down the road from us.

There was a long wait. Gurus tend to be fashionably late, and I think it builds the tension a bit so that there is a high sense of anticipation and devotional energy when they enter the room. But that's all part of the pageant and fun.

When Sharavana Baba stepped into the room, he took a few paces up and down, then walked directly over to Jane, sitting on a chair at the back, and placed a pink rose in her hand. Then he walked to the front of the room, where I was sitting with the others on the floor, patted me on the head and touched my hand. I think everyone wondered what was going on—including us. We were the only people in the room he did this to. There were a few other westerners in the room, so how did he know that Jane and I were a couple? I hadn't even seen him walk into the room since I was looking toward the front. The first I knew was the friendly touch to the head and the thought running across my mind: "So nice to see you. Sorry for the wait." Jane had been thinking about the perennial problems with our children when Sharavana Baba gave her the rose.

What struck me with Sharavana Baba was how jolly he was. When we conferred afterwards, Jane and I both thought he looked like our daughter's first husband, who was a thick-set man with a swastika and prison tattoos all over his face and shaven head. This man was the exact opposite: kind, gentle, and radiating love. It felt a bit like a cosmic joke as Sharavana Baba sat in his seat and bounced around to the *bhajans*, whimsically twirling flowers. He was clearly a man who liked to have fun. Jane and I were both immediately enchanted by him. You could see he was a realized being who radiated joy. It was definitely worth missing the Sunday roast and the shopping trip.

Sharavana Baba spoke mainly Malayalam, which was translated into short and simple statements in English. He held up a tangerine and gave a simple but inspiring talk about the importance of the inner life and how, like the fruit, the outside may be beautiful, but the inside has the vitamin C—something you need but cannot see. He went on to talk about how if we focus on the inner life and get that right, then everything in our world outside will get better, too. It was much the same sort of message that other gurus teach but expressed beautifully and straightforwardly, with lots of happy smiles and jokes in between.

I never trust gurus who are too serious. For me, one of the marks of enlightenment is humour mixed with humility, for it is only the ego that takes itself so seriously.

At the end of the proceedings, everyone waited in line in front of Sharavana Baba in his golden chair to be given a personal interview. We were quite close to the front of the line and could see various people expressing their worries and distress and getting comfort from the guru. Knowing how draining it can be to work with people's spiritual problems and to give clairvoyant guidance, we could see that Sharavana Baba had a pretty daunting task on his hands, but he appeared never to tire. From the little one could overhear, it was clear that he was giving much more than general advice but was giving detailed and personal insights into people's lives.

The lady in front of Jane and me was very distressed but walked away comforted. When Jane and I kneeled together before him, a silly mood set in immediately. It was like talking to an old friend whom you've known for years and whom you can rib a bit and pull their leg. To me, it felt as if all three of us were sharing a hilarious joke. Yet, during the conversation between the three of us, he was simultaneously talking directly to Jane and directly to me. It all took about fifteen minutes, but that short time was hugely mind-opening.

He told both of us that we were very old souls and had more spiritual work to do. "You have visited many gurus now and in your time, and because of this you can meet people like me, and we all can be happy. The last time was two years ago"—which we took to mean the meeting with the guru I mentioned earlier, which bothered Jane and nearly prevented her from coming along.

He said that we had all been together before in past lives. "Where's the rose I gave you?" he said to Jane. As she replied, "In my bag," Sharavana Baba gave me a sideways, cheeky glance. The two of us, preempting what obviously should follow, simultaneously said, "It's in her heart!" As he spoke, he lightly nudged his head against my forehead like two people sharing a joyous moment. "It's in my heart, too," he said.

He looked back at me and said, "You have nothing to worry about with your family." Then he turned to Jane and said, "Stop worrying about your children," which had been a big concern of Jane, not only that day but in the weeks and months before. For me, too, there had been a lot of health worries in the family of late. He spoke again to me, saying, "You have been held back for a long time." Turning to Jane, he said, "And you know your husband here has a great deal of spiritual work in store, starting at the age sixty-two, and there will be a lot of travel, too—for both of you."

These words were almost a paraphrase of the exact words written on my Naadi leaves and an important confirmation of the prophecies. "You do not have to chase it. It will find you," he advised.

I told him that this was what the Naadi leaves had predicted for me and asked him if he knew anything about my past life. He explained that I had been with

Shirdi Sai Baba and also knew Sri Ramakrishna. (I thought he said Ramana Maharshi, as there was a lot of noise around, but Jane corrects me here.) He said I had been a devotee of Shiva in my former lives and lived at a Shiva temple in Tamil South India. (I missed the name, as it was too hard to pronounce and recall.) Again, this corresponded very closely with the Naadi message I had recently had and hoped to get confirmed from an independent spiritual channel.

He beamed a big smile and said, "I *am* the Naadi!"

Our eyes met, and I chuckled: "So am I. I guess we all are!" (Words that came out of I don't know where.) We all joked together a little more, and he concluded our interview with an invitation to his ashram in Kerala.

"You MUST come to my ashram in Kerala. Will you do that?"

"Yes", says Jane.

A week later, we had a second opportunity to meet Sharavana Baba on Easter Sunday at a private house in London. By now, word had spread among the Indian population, and the small house was packed to the ceiling with people. I had hoped to ask the swami some specific questions about mediumship and the afterlife. Unlike most Spiritualists, I believe the next life is not the final destination, and I wanted to ask him—as I had asked other gurus—what his take was on what happens after death. It looked like I would not get the opportunity.

The evening was conducted mainly in Tamil, with a short discourse in English about the primary meaning of the teachings of Jesus and our spiritual place in this garden we call Earth. There were some prayers and *bhajans* (chanted, repetitive Indian songs), and then everyone was invited for a short interview. Again he beamed his lovely smile, hugged and patted us both, repeating again his earlier messages about the spiritual happiness we have and will share with the world.

Jane and Craig meeting Sharavana in London

There was no opportunity to ask detailed questions, as a large crowd was pressing for his attention. When we got home, I flicked open one of his books that I'd bought, and the answer to the question I had intended to put to him about the transitory nature of Heaven was there in black and white: "As for the enjoyment of Heaven, it is also subject to impermanence, frustration, and failure. The sacrifices that propitiate the gods entitle the sacrificer to the same heavenly pleasures as the gods themselves enjoy, but only for as long as the fruits of his merits last. Thereafter he takes birth in the lower regions, according to his past actions and associations. So long as they are propelled by the *gunas*, the senses are active, they perceive diversity in the *atman* and impel action, the fruits of action, and bondage for the individual."

What was remarkable about the early meetings with Sharavana Baba was that he seemed to know and anticipate our thoughts. What made it all so hilarious was that Jane and I also have pronounced telepathic skills, so it all became a wonderful cosmic joke of anticipating each other's thoughts. I'm not sure if it felt quite the same for Jane, but I sensed we'd all connected inwardly, and there was a childlike game happening, where we were all trying to be the first one to catch the thoughts floating in the air. Impossible to describe, really, but some of the mediums reading this may get what I mean.

Sharavana Baba not only knew and was able to preempt questions in our minds, but just as on the previous occasion, he held three intimate conversations simultaneously: with Jane, with me, and between the three of us together. Something was happening on a much deeper level than anyone observing the events could have recognized. Jane and I walked away from the interviews in a spiritual daze and felt very inspired and cosmically charged.

We saw him for the third time when he visited the Crawley Amman temple near London. The discourse was in Tamil, but we could talk to him briefly afterwards in English, with occasional help from a translator. To me, he said: "You are at the turning point, and both of you are now on a divine path." Then he turned to Jane and, with a mischievous and funny look in his eyes, said: "How's your family? Now happy with family? Very, very happy?"

Since our last visit, our daughter Danielle announced her engagement to an intelligent, loyal, and handsome Italian "god" and became pregnant. In the past, she had undergone some horrendous ordeals, but now she was very, very happy, not just with the planned baby and marriage, but also since she had been told by the doctors after having her first baby, Willow, that it would be extremely unlikely she would ever have another child. Some time ago, Jane, Danielle, and I had all simultaneously dreamed on the same night of Sathya Sai Baba talking to us at Danielle's house and telling us that he would sort everything out. Now here was the same light shining through Sharavana Baba.

Sharavana Baba handed Jane a rose and, pointing to the stem, said, "Life has a few thorns, but as you can see, they are not much compared to the beauty of the flower. And just like a rose, you will always retain your beauty."

CHAPTER 3

Mystic Journey

Not long after the first meetings with Sadhguru Sri Sharavana Baba, I went to India to do the Naadi remedies that would clear the karma from my past lives and allow the positive predictions made in the Naadi to happen. This quest involved my travelling all over India doing puja in temples, Homan fire rituals and visiting a miraculous yogi called Maha Ananda Siddha—a man who could sleep in burning coals and is said will live for another 200 years. I took a cameraman friend with me. With the guidance of film producer Louis Frost, we made our extraordinary adventures into a movie called *'Mystic Journey to India'*. (Amazon Prime.)

Doing the Naadi remedies involved travelling thousands of miles back and forth across Southern India. I performed many ceremonial activities in the temples, climbed and walked around Mount

Arunachala and did lots of charitable work. The Naadi remedies instructed me to feed the poor in remote villages, feed the children at an orphanage and give cows to destitute senior citizens. It was an extraordinary journey and a deeply moving experience. I met sadhus and holy men, visited sacred sites and was invited to study the Naadi leaves. All this, I feel, connected me to the ancient knowledge of India and is something that will forever stay with me.

We saw some spectacular scenery and grand temples, mangroves and ancient sites, but the most beautiful experience of all was happening inside me. As each of the Naadi remedies was completed, I could feel transformations happening inside my soul. I had cleared my karma, and now a new destiny awaited me.

I returned exhausted and with the beginnings of septicemia (blood poisoning), which was immediately treated in the UK and caught before it could harm. But our adventures had been amazing, and we had extraordinary film footage in the can that our director Louis Frost could now edit.

There had been no time to visit Sharavana Baba's ashram at Sreekrishnapuram. We travelled mainly between Chennai, Rameswaram and Kanyakumari, which is a long way from Kerala.

Cannes Film Festival

It took about a year to edit our movie *Mystic Journey to India*. A large part of it had been shot in 4K on a high-resolution RED camera. We had no dedicated sound person or crew on location, so it was a huge task to pull it all together and make a cohesive story that could grip the viewer. We were also working with massive files, and our antiquated PCs and Apple Macs struggled to process everything. Eventually, it was complete and just in time for our Canadian distributor to present it at the Cannes MIPCOM festival in France. As Sharavana Baba says: "Failure is easy, but success is hard! Strive for victory!"

Jane and I headed for the Cannes Festival to help with the promotion and to network with some of the contacts our American agent Marina had given us. We stayed in the nearby town of Nice, close to the Promenade des Anglais where the 2016 terrorist attack happened. It brings it home to stand where the carnage had occurred at the spot that I had 'seen' with my prophecy in 2015 when I made my predictions about what would happen. To stand at the site where so many had died brings the horror of the event home.

Cannes was an exciting, swish and optimistic but also a very materialistic place. Everywhere were gaudy posters and advertising hoardings plastered with adverts for the next blockbusters. Clearly, it was going to be very hard to sell a spiritual film about holy India. From the fierce marketing all around us, it was clear that everyone wants trashy entertainment and remakes of ideas that have already been done. There were some very dark souls here, too.

"Did you hear what that man on the next table was talking about?" hissed Jane under her breath. "He's having an affair and also had a Russian prostitute last night. Now he has the audacity to call his wife on his cell phone."

"Lower your voice," I say as I gulp down the overpriced food, "You'll get us kicked out."

"But it's disgusting," continued Jane, now turning round to look at the table behind us. "On that table, men were saying that they slept with three girls each last night and on the table over there…" And so on. This place was a den of iniquity but a fabulous place if you like to eavesdrop.

Jane nearly throttled two arrogant potential buyers of the film when they boasted and joked to one another about their sexual antics away from their wives at home. That meeting didn't go well. How can you sell a spiritual movie to these disgusting men?

Cannes was awash with money and bad values in equal measure. We returned home without closing a sale but, despite everything, did also make some good contacts. Meanwhile, our distributor had a stand in the main festival areas and generated much interest in the movie.

The problem we encountered was that what we had to sell was utterly different from anything they'd seen before. People loved the feature version when they watched screenings, but it was hard for the interested channels to find a suitable slot for it. The movie wasn't quite entertainment, and it wasn't quite documentary. It was a three-part series, and most channels were looking for six parts and, of course, there were a lot of 'hungry dogs' here all 'chasing the one bone'. It was a ferocious battle to sell into the available air time, and we only had limited contacts and no marketing budget.

Bhrigu Samhita

On our return, I contacted my friend Sri Saktibaanee in Denmark and arranged to get a prediction about the movie from the Bhrigu Samhita. This is similar to the Naadi, except it is an astrological oracle. You ask six questions but do not have to give your thumbprint to access the oracle as it has an index that has the names of everyone who will consult it together with the time and date they will ask. These appointments were set up thousands of years ago. The Bhruguji Prashna Samhita is another little known wonder of India.

Maharishi Bhrigu writing through the manuscript told us that the film would sell later, gave the times of the next Cannes festival and advised, "Everything will come automatically to him when the time and circumstances are right. It is due to his stubbornness that he, at times, has suffered in his career." Interestingly, this is the same thing Sharavana Baba had said to me when we last briefly spoke to him at a public event.

The oracle also gave me some remedies, one of which included performing the Batuk Bhairava puja, chanting Om Namo Bhagavate Vasudevaya and feeding birds at special times. However, there were also other things said in the text not connected to the film project that worried me a little. It said: "There may be a desperate or serious health problem within the family circle but still by the Grace of God also many things will come to happen. Overall it is seen that he will achieve his ambitions step by step, and the only real worry is related to his family and some members there, but also that will come to a solution."

I was unsure whom this prophecy related to. There were some serious health problems in the family, but elsewhere in the prediction, it seemed to hint that this was a direct blood link. Who was this referring to?

Some months later, I had my answer when our grandchild Damian (aged 2) was rushed into hospital as we arrived for a family day out at a steampunk festival. My daughter, Danielle, and her partner, Domenico, dashed to the hospital while we took Damian's sister, Willow, around the show and tried not to look worried.

Later my daughter called my mobile and, with a choked voice, said, "It's bad news Dad. Damian has Type 1 Diabetes."

CHAPTER 4

The Shock Sinks in

Most people do not know how serious is Type 1 Diabetes. I didn't. When it was diagnosed and explained to Danielle and Domenico, they both cried. I always confused it with type 2 diabetes which, in my arrogance, I would class as a serves-you-right fat person's disease. Type 2 Diabetes, we assume, is caused by gluttony, lack of exercise and too much sugar. Today with lax food laws and greedy manufacturers, it's hard to avoid excess sugars and fats—today, one-third of the world's population is obese or overweight, so Type 2 could hit any of us.

Many of us sit in front of computers all day, TV and social media at night, and just about everything we eat is loaded with vast amounts of sugar. The big corporations con us by serving us crappy processed food and disguise the bland taste of the cheap, unhealthy ingredients by loading it with sugar. They trick us with words such as 'light', meaning that it's low in fat—oh, that's good for me—but loaded with your whole daily sugar requirement. It is becoming increasingly hard to eat anything today without filling your veins with treacle.

Diabetes is also prevalent. In the United States, more than one in every ten adults who are 20 years or older has diabetes. There, 29.1 million people in the United States have it, and 8.1 million may be undiagnosed. About 10% of people with diabetes have Type 1 diabetes.

Type 1 Diabetes

Fortunately, type 2 diabetes can be combated through lifestyle changes. If a person has a persistent diet, does lots of exercises and introduces lifestyle changes, they can lower A1c's to a level deemed "non-diabetic". This has to be a permanent lifestyle change, or the diabetes returns. It's not curable as such, but it can be reversed.

Sadly this is not the case with Type 1 Diabetes. This is a chronic condition in which the pancreas produces little or no insulin. Insulin is a hormone needed to allow sugar (glucose) to enter cells to produce energy. In Damian's case, his pancreas is shot to pieces. Type 1 diabetes is an autoimmune condition. It's caused by the body attacking its own pancreas with antibodies. In children like Damian, the damaged pancreas doesn't make insulin. It is a lifelong condition.

Managing a child with Type 1 Diabetes is a steep learning curve. Fortunately, both Danielle and Domenico are intelligent and sensible people, but I don't know how some less well-educated people cope. I couldn't. For a start, I'm needle-phobic and pass out at the sight of an injection or blood. One of the most horrible times I recall was when I had to have a blood transfusion in hospital. I felt traumatized.

Managing Type 1 Diabetes gets easier, they say, but at first, it was a full-on 24/7 battle just to keep Damian alive. Before every meal, his blood has to be tested and ketones measured. Then his food has to be weighed, and the exact amount of sugar in it worked out. Once you know how much sugar is in a meal, Damian is injected with the precise amount of insulin to balance it out. But of course, he's only two and may decide that he's not going to eat or maybe eat everything and more. He may bolt it down or pick at his food over two hours. Kids of two years old are finicky. You may have noticed this.

If he eats too little, you have to feed him extra sugar with something like apple juice. If he eats too much, you inject him with more insulin. This balancing act goes on for every meal and snack with additional tests through the night if his ketones change unexpectedly. If he runs around a lot, his sugars burn up quickly, and he needs to be checked. If you take him from a warm indoors to cold outdoors, you check. If he falls asleep suddenly, you check in case he's lapsed into a coma. He could lose a limb or his sight. Damian lives in a world of constant pinpricks.

Despite the constant care, there were emergencies with late-night dashes to the hospital by car or ambulance. There was no let-up and not much help from the hospital. Essential monitoring equipment that Damian needed was not supplied, and there was a six-week wait for it. This meant that either Danielle or Domenico had to sit up all night taking blood on the hour. If they fell asleep, Damian could go into a coma.

In the morning, they would take Willow (age 9) to school, Domenico would make his two-hour drive to work and do a job that requires full concentration. They were getting no sleep at all. It was an impossible situation.

Jane and I felt helpless. There was very little we could do to help. But maybe I could do something: Perhaps I could get some advice from the Naadi. Is there some karmic cause to all this? What if I could find Damian's Naadi? Maybe there's a remedy there to help him?

CHAPTER 5

The Naadi Remedies

I'd consulted the Naadi in the past to find a cure for my cluster headaches. For about a year I was having sudden and debilitating headaches and seemed to be getting nowhere with the doctors. I arranged a consultation with the Bhrigu Samhita, which gave me an unusual remedy. I had to walk to the local river every day for a few weeks, say a mantra and empty a small packet of flour in the water. At a set time I then made a mixture of ginger, three types of peppers, Curcumin and ground ivory on my forehead. (I had an old ivory knife that I ground down.)

I sat around with this weird cadmium yellow mush on my forehead for the prescribed three days. The stains won't come off clothes or my face. My friends and family—and anyone I met in public—really did believe that I had some horrible outbreak of jaundice. No matter how hard I scrubbed, the yellow stains would not go. I'd walk around Sainsbury's looking like the living dead—a Homer zombie from the Simpson's *Treehouse of Horror*. I refused to accept Jane's suggestion to wear a bag over my head, so I just pretended to be ill—or facially challenged.

Remarkably, the remedy worked. I couldn't believe what had happened. I had a blinding headache in my temples while I mixed the potion, but the headache disappeared as soon as it touched my skin. "This must be a placebo effect," I muttered to myself. Nonetheless, my blinding headaches vanished and—apart from one or two very mild attacks—have never returned.

This potion is not the cure for cluster headaches, as these Naadi remedies are different for everyone. Someone else asking about the same problem will get a completely different remedy. This treatment is not medicine in the western sense because the cure works on the karmic and spiritual level.

If the Naadis could do this for my debilitating condition, then maybe something could be done for Damian? Initially, I had a chat with my friend and Naadi reader, Mr Prakash. He had a look at Damian's horoscope, and what he saw concerned him. He suggested that we organize an Ayush Homam. This ritual is a fire ceremony performed for health and long life. In India, the tradition is usually performed on every family member's birthday and a child's first birthday.

I didn't want to consult the Naadi through Mr Prakash. I had already told him about Damian's condition and needed verification from an independent source that knew nothing about the situation. I trust my friend implicitly, but they might think I'd been tricked if I were to show the Naadi to others. Instead, I asked Sri Saktibaanee for help and asked him to make sure that the Naadi reader was told absolutely nothing about Damian's condition.

Craig searches for the Naadi in India

Agastya Jeeva Naadi

We would consult the Agastya Jeeva Naadi that I mentioned in chapter 1. Sri Saktibaanee had been consulting it over many years and was working on a book about it. I would write the foreword. At that time, we were waiting for the Jeeva Naadi to give permission to publish its revelations.

Something remarkable had been spoken through this miraculous oracle that has blank leaves, which relay written messages as the question is asked. The Naadi reader was Hanumathan Dasan, whom Sri Saktibaanee had consulted on many occasions. One day while he was waiting for his next client, the leaves began writing messages in light. These were communications coming directly from the great Tamil Saint Maha Guru Agastya. He has used the Naadi to reveal information and remedies based on astrology and the Ramayana to help anyone to eradicate the effects of their bad karma.

Agastya, who was communicating through the palm leaves, was one of the eighteen Siddhas. A 'Siddha is a person who has realized the non-duality of the Jivatma. They are God-realized beings who have also conquered time and had/have the ability to know everything that will ever happen. Agastya and the Siddhas are the authors of the Naadi, and they are the ones who help us know our destiny and eradicate the negative effects of past life karma to set us on the road to salvation. Agastya was the first disciple of Shiva.

He attained Samadhi at Ananthashayana but people believe that he still lives on. Some say he appears in physical form and others say he communicates from the astral plane. I presume he has attained an omnipresent state—like Sathya Sai Baba—and works on all planes of existence. However, now he was communicating directly to us through the Jeeva Naadi.

The communications told of many mysterious things hinted at in the text such as the stories about the Siddhas, the Sanjeevani art and the secrets of eternal life. The Naadi reader Hanumathan Dasan realized that a very important spiritual work was coming through the leaves. The most important part was the teachings about the fifth chapter of Valmiki's Ramayana that we were told can be chanted as remedies for overcoming any problems in life. The chapter tells of the adventures of Hanuman, his journey to Lanka to rescue Sita, and of his selflessness, strength, and devotion to Rama.

Agastya reveals the deeper meanings of this holy text—the *Sukham Tharum Sundara Kandam*—and how the verses can be used as specific remedies for every complaint or problem imaginable. The Sundara Kandam is traditionally read before the rest of the Ramayana. Its recital brings harmony to the household. The Jeeva Naadi messages expanded on this tradition, giving us specific passages that can help to remove particular obstacles. The act of reading these passages triggers powerful and transformative forces in the reader's life.

Agastya permitted the book to be published. It is called *"Maha Guru Agastya—Sukham Tharum Sundra Kandam. The Book of Perfect Healing and Happiness"* Sri Saktibaanee asked me to write a foreword, and the book is now available on Amazon.

When I was sent a draft copy of this remarkable manuscript, I was struck by some of the first words transcribed: "There will always be someone looking for something good to happen. And for their good wishes to happen, they should seek the blessings of Lord Murugan. Yes, this is a very simple source and truth. Agastya Muni conducted the first Chathru Samhara Yaga (Holy offering ceremony) in Panchesti as per the orders of Lord Murugan and in the presence of Goddess Gauri.

Many types of mantras are mentioned, but the foremost that makes one's wishes come true is the "Subramanya Moola Mantra Thrishadhi" slokas. Lord Subramanya Moola Mantra: OM SHREEM HREEM VREEM SOWM SARAVANABHAVA."

Murugan and the Naadi

After consulting the Agastya Jeeva Naadi for Damian, it was only much later that I realized the close connection here with Murugan. I contacted Sri Saktibaanee by email, and he arranged for a search to be done for Damian's Naadi Predictions. We made sure that no mention was made in any correspondence of Damian's Type 1 Diabetes. No matter how trustworthy the source, I always insist that the Naadi reader has no clues. This way, we can prove to those with a sceptical mindset and ourselves that the naadi is the real deal.

I asked my daughter, Danielle (Damian's mum), for permission to open his Naadi. I explained that I hoped to find some guidance about Damian's illness, but also we must be prepared as the Naadi can sometimes be brutal in what it says. Foremost in my mind was the memory of asking the Naadi for help with my sister's partner. I'd asked the Naadi for guidance about his terrible illness that lingered for over two years. The Naadi said that the illness was part of his Prarabdha Karma. This is karma that cannot be reversed and must be experienced through the present body (incarnation). In other words, there was no remedy, and it said that all we could do was pray for him. He died without a remedy being given.

I will not quote all of the predictions about Damian given by the Agastya Naadi as some must remain private. However, what is relevant to this story and what leapt off the page were these harrowing words:

"Neither does he have good physical health. He will have a short life." It said some more things and then, "He will suffer from a very serious disease called Prameha Pida. (A serious diabetic disorder.) But if he soon comes in contact with any Sadhu/Monk and gets the blessings, then he will complete his life period up to late age."

I was shocked to read this, and there was more in the predictions that gave me concern when it reaffirmed that his life was in danger, but it also had a hopeful note that it is possible to meet this Sadhu/Monk. It said, "Now presently, this is the period when such a very happy incident may take place; this with the good help of some family-related person of his, meaning that there is a great chance of meeting any Guru or Sadhu. This lucky period is from now on until June this year 2018. Here, with the help of some good and spiritual person, he shall seek to meet any Guru or Monk, and by that, a heavy burden will be taken away from his shoulders."

Other remedies were given, but clearly, this was the most important and pressing. Jane and I were not regular devotees of Sharavana Baba. We had visited him only four times at public events since our first meetings described earlier. Again, he had given us some interesting advice and encouragement with our spiritual work. I had given him a copy of my book *'Messages from the Universe'* in which I described our earlier meeting. He was thrilled. I remember his saying that Jane and I were like two broad trees under which many people could shelter. It was a lovely image that stuck in my mind. Again he looked at Jane and urged us to come to Kerala.

Damian's Naadi reading had been transcribed into English by Kim and sent to me by email. Moments before receiving it, I idly looked at my phone and accidentally opened the Sharavana Baba "app" for the first time and noticed that Sharavana Baba was visiting London soon. Of course, when I read in the Naadi that we must see a Sadhu/Monk before June, I immediately thought of the Sharavana Baba app that I'd been looking at and frantically checked again to see if the dates corresponded with the Naadi.

It was now late March 2018, and the Naadi was saying that we needed to see a holy man before June if we were to break the spell for Damian. Seeing a godly man is easy if you live in India but a 'tall order' in the UK. To add to the urgency, we were soon to fly to Barcelona so time was at a premium. If he was available, we would have to see Sharavana Baba immediately.

CHAPTER 6

Seeking a Holy Man

How do you explain to a sceptical daughter that her son's life is in danger but can be extended if he sees a holy man within the next few days? Our daughter, Danielle, has never been kind to religion. "It's a teddy bear for the weak-minded", she would often say or "Religion is for delusional people." On so many levels, I agree with her. I, too, argue that beliefs can be destructive and have also cited the argument that just because we may believe that a chocolate teapot is orbiting the Sun does not necessarily mean it is true. Just like Danielle, I am not a subscriber to the 'man in the sky' version of God.

On one level, she was absolutely right, of course, but this was not my view. What she attacks is the dualist idea that God is something separate from creation. The opposite argument to the non-dualist idea is that everything is God, including us. Of course, there are also shades in between—maybe both ideas are correct depending on our spiritual viewpoint. How could I explain to Danielle that there is an omnipresent state—a supreme spirit—that has many forms, pervades the whole universe and contains everything to include creation and destruction, male and female, good and evil, movement and stillness and so on.

There was no time for philosophical discussion. I would simply have to show her the Naadi reading and let her make her own decision. It felt like a cruel thing to do, particularly as it said it would take a miracle for Damian to live past five. Dealing with so many emergencies and crises was tough enough, and I didn't want to add another sword of Damocles to her troubles. But how could I live with not saying something? The Naadi had foreseen the future, but it had also offered a remedy, so it would be irresponsible not to act upon it.

Danielle knew about my interest in the Naadi. It had been hard to stop me from talking about it, and, as she knew, I had written many books about it. I handed her the transcript. "It makes frightening reading but don't panic," I said. "the Naadi lays bare the future, but it also offers some remedies to change things."

Her face dropped when she read it. "So what do we have to do?" she asked.

I was relieved to see that she had not completely rejected the idea.

"First, we must see the sadhu/monk that it mentions. Afterwards, I will get all the other remedies done myself or in India," I replied. "But time is pressing. The holy man that Mum and I saw some time ago is visiting London this week, but he's going back to Kerala very soon. We need to go ASAP."

We checked our diaries. Danielle's was packed with crucial hospital appointments for Damian, and school commitments for her other child Willow and Jane and I were flying to Barcelona after that. There was only one day we had available: Tuesday 15th March 2018.

I checked the app. Sharavana Baba was in London that day, but it was a public event. Jane and I knew from experience that this would not be easy for Damian. Sharavana Baba would appear for what the Hindus call darshan. Darshan is a Sanskrit word meaning 'sight,' 'vision', or 'appearance.' At public events like these, Sharavana Baba will arrive after hours of preparation. The congregation will sit on the floor or on seats, Bhajans (sacred songs) will be sung, and eventually, Sharavana Baba will walk around the hall and give a talk. At the very end of the proceedings, Sharavana Baba will speak to everybody one by one for a minute or two. You are given a numbered ticket for the queue when you first arrive. From arriving to the point when you sit with Sharavana Baba can take many hours of patient waiting.

"Damian could never cope with a public event," groaned Jane. "He wouldn't be able to keep still, and his sugar levels will be all over the place. He has trouble with long journeys too. He couldn't manage it all."

I called the number on the app, and fortunately, there was a solution. I was told that Sharavana Baba also gave private meetings. These cost £201 that all go to his charitable trust, which goes to help the needy in India.

"We are all set. We can go on Tuesday," I said as I came off the phone. "He'll see us in the morning and just before the public event."

The Beast from the East

It was fortunate that Sharavana Baba could see us on the only day we had available, but there seemed to be another problem in our way. The night before we were to travel, the television news announced that Britain would be hit by an unprecedented snowstorm coming in from Russia. They called it the 'Beast from the East', and the news told everyone not to travel.

Forecasters issued red weather warnings of a danger to life. The storm's 70mph winds would hit the polar vortex bringing deadly snowdrifts and a minus 15°C wind-chill in some areas. The message was clear: do not travel.

Canadians, Swedes, Norwegians, and the rest laugh at how Britain stops when there's a flutter of snow, but this storm was different. The whole country came to a standstill. The Guardian newspaper estimates that the disruption caused by 'Beast from the East' cost the UK economy £1 billion a day.

Despite the dire weather warnings, we drove to London and encountered hardly any snow on our journey. The country was at a standstill, but somehow it missed the M3 motorway. I have experienced this sort of thing before: The way ahead becomes clear when you set off on a journey of significant spiritual importance. It was an easy journey all the way with bright sunshine. On the way home, too, our journey was pretty well snow-free. All the other motorways across the country were snowbound.

"Are you sure that this is a good idea?" asked Danielle from the back as she gave Damian a shot of insulin after he'd been car sick. "With religion and gurus and the rest, people con themselves. They are so desperate to believe that they hear what they want to hear and see what they want to see. It's all delusional stuff."

"You don't have to believe anything," I replied. "Roll with it and see what happens. There's nothing to lose and maybe he'll prove something to you. They say that if you have a question in your mind, he'll answer it before you can ask."

Jane changed the subject. "It's amazing how you're getting to grips with managing Damian's diabetes. Working out the carbs before any snack or meal, planning his meals and checking if his sugars drop if he's been running around a lot… it all takes some doing."

"And the hospitals and support literature are terrible," replied Danielle. "Everything is geared up for adults with Type 2 Diabetes; there's not much intelligent help available for Type 1 and next to nothing out there to help with babies and toddlers.

"My carb count meal book shows mainly calorie counts for adult meals. I have to half the numbers for Damian, and that's assuming he'll eat everything. And if they're ill or car sick, or whatever, you have to recalculate everything. I'm sure some mums must get desperate. That's why I'm thinking of writing a guidebook for mothers with diabetic kids."

"What a brilliant idea!" exclaimed Jane. "I'm sure you could do that. You and Domenico really know your stuff now."

"It would be about how to manage diabetes if you have a young child. And maybe it would help me to get an income so that we can save some money and get our own big house one day."

We arrive at the London 'ashram'—which sounds very grandiose but in reality, is a small flat above a post office in the Harrow area of London. Below is an oversized garage converted to a temple. For public events, this is extended by removing the cars and waste bins and attaching a marquee over the parking area.

There's no signage except for a wheel clamping warning for the businesses next door. We worked out that the ashram must be at the top of the iron fire escape to the side of the garage/temple.

Danielle looked a bit shocked. "The crazy things you and mum take me to," she said as we got out of the car.

"This reminds me of when I was about seven, and we all went to a house to buy an Ouija board that mum had seen advertised in the paper. Or maybe that time when I was looked after by your friends when you went to see Sai Baba for two weeks in India. Or perhaps that time you sent me to a playschool run by nutty born again Christians. Or maybe when you dragged us all to see the Dalai Lama…"

Clearly, Danielle was resisting just a little as she reeled off more as we ascended the snow-covered iron staircase and knocked on the door to the ashram.

CHAPTER 7

The London Ashram

We were greeted by an Indian lady and squeezed past her into a small kitchen area adjoining the main room. The whole place was filled with thick smoke and the smell of incense. There was melodic chanting coming from the front room. I glimpsed someone holding a small lighted oil diva lamp.

"They are doing the Arti ceremony," I explained with confidence as we sat in an adjacent small room and waited until we were called to see Sharavana Baba. Damian was running around, opening draws, rearranging flowers and pleased to be out of the car seat. Keeping him still is like juggling with eels. "Arti is just a few oil lamps on a tray. It is a greeting ceremony offered to the gods and also sometimes to gurus and holy people," I said as I pulled Damian away from the telephone with its tempting buttons.

Eventually, someone called us so we could now

meet Sharavana Baba in the main room. We pulled Damian away from the collection plate that he found on the table and stepped into the smoky room.

I was wrong about Arti. What they'd been doing was a Havan. This ritual is a fire ceremony done over a small grate made from house bricks arranged in the centre of the room. A Havan is a religious ceremony performed in temples that involves worship through the use of a sacred fire. The use of fire as a means of worship is the most ancient of all rites, going back to the earliest Vedic times.

This situation reminded me of my time in India, not only because I had participated in many of these rituals but also because of their endearing disregard for fire regulations. It's not often you see an open fire in the middle of an upstairs living room above a post office, and the windows propped open to let out the billowing fumes. No wonder it was so smoky!

Sharavana Baba sits on the floor with his back against the wall and faces an altar heavily laden with flowers, candles, fruits, grains, pictures, and statues of gods and goddesses. He smiles at us through the smoke haze. Someone near us puts a little scented water into our palm and marks each of our foreheads with a turmeric paste mark. Danielle looks puzzled, "What do I do with the water?"

Before I have time to explain that the mark is a Tilaka—worn as a mark of honour and welcome to guests, or that the water is holy water to be drunk, we are called over to sit beside Sharavana Baba. He was pleased to see us and held our hands. Sharavana Baba does not speak a lot of English, and usually, there's a translator present, but he gets his messages across with simple language.

"Very happy you come here," he says. He turns to me. "It is good to write books. It is a spiritual task. It is good to write books. You can reach people, and sometimes it can really help people on the path."

He asks me to tell him about what I am writing, and he is pleased to hear what I say and gives me encouragement. He told me that I sometimes feel restricted by writing all the time and yearn to spend more time working in the real world and demonstrating mediumship, lecturing, inspiring people and so on.

"Your spiritual life is going well?' he says to Jane and me. "Very well," replies Jane.

Jane has been helping a lot of people through readings, and she feels that sometimes Sharavana Baba's energy is behind the upsurge in interest. It's as if he sends them.

"You are very busy with your spiritual work now," he says to Jane. He mentions a number of other things about our lives that were correct, which I will not reproduce here. He then turns to Danielle, who is still wrestling with Damian and trying to stop his grabbing the candles and fruit from the nearby altar.

"You have a good marriage," he says. "For now, you stay in the house where you are now. "Sometimes you argue, but most times it is good. Your husband has a good job. He is a good businessman too. One day you will have a big house." Sharavana Baba appeared to be aware of the fact that Danielle and her partner Domenico were renting and hoping to get their own place. We had been discussing this in the car during the journey to London.

"Don't be sad," he continued. You are a very strong person. I know you do not believe. It is okay to have doubts. You are like a spiritual mother. You should pray on Fridays to God in the form of the mother."

Sharavana Baba looks to Jane and says, "It is good that you also look after your mother," and resumes speaking to Danielle. "Don't forget to look after your mother too."

He pats Dannielle fondly and says, "Don't worry about your son. I will look after him. From today you will gradually begin to live a spiritual life."

"You are not working?" he asks. "You should write!" We were all surprised by this as he again answered the questions that we had been talking about moments earlier during the drive to London. You will remember that I had warned Danielle that Sharavana Baba would answer her questions before she could ask them.

He reaches out and holds the hands of Jane and me. "Your health good?" he asks.

"Yes were are fine," we reply.

"Still happy?"

"Yes." I then explained to Sharavana Baba that we were here because of a message in the Agastya Jeeva Naadi that had told us to bring our grandchild to see him on this day.

"The Naadi is always correct," he says. "Five thousand years ago, they saw this day. I came to England this time especially to see your grandchild." (A devotee later confirmed this.)

"He was a Brahmin. His spiritual name is Hari Shankara. This means half Vishnu and half Shiva." (This god is usually known as Harihara and sometimes as Shankaranarayana. Shankara is Shiva, and Narayana is Vishnu.)

He asked us to put Damian on his lap, and Damian stops wriggling about and sits quietly. Sharavana Baba talks about Damian for a while and then starts singing the Gayatri Mantra with a tone reminiscent of children's lullaby.

Om bhur bhuvah svah
tatsaviturvarenyam
bhargo devasyadhimahi
dhiyo yo nah pracodayat

I know this mantra from the Rigveda so join in the chanting. Damian liked it, and I noticed that Damian counted his fingers to the beat of the meter in the way someone would chant japa without mala beads. The mantra is a call to awakening. Swami Vivekananda translates it as "We meditate on the glory of that Being who has produced this universe; may He enlighten our minds."

Sharavana Baba's choice of mantra was significant as one of the remedies in Damian's Naadi says: "He should arrange for the chanting of the Gayatri Mantra to be chanted 125,000 times by Brahmin priests. With this, he will enjoy a good life." Of all the mantras Sharavana Baba could have spoken, he chose the same mantra prescribed in the Naadi. When these powerful mantras are chanted over a period of time, the qualities of the mantra rub off on us. We take on the qualities of the gods we incant.

Sharavana Baba intuitively knew that this was in the Naadi. When he'd finished chanting, he looked at me and said, "Your mantra is Namah Shivaya." Again this was significant as my Naadi had said the same thing to me years ago. This mantra is the

Panchakshara mantra that I chant every day and for an extended period on a Monday. It literally means "five letters" in Sanskrit and refers to the five holy letters 'Na', 'Ma', 'Si', 'Va', 'Ya'.

One of my most important Naadi remedies was to chant this 108 times per day for 144 days and then have the mantra engraved on a noble metal foil. This personal mantra has been reaffirmed multiple times in many of the Naadis I have consulted. Again Sharavana Baba knew my mantra.

CHAPTER 8

Cosmic Trance

When the Gayatri Mantra is finished, Damian jumps off Sharavana Baba's lap and scrambles over to the altar to blow at the candle flames. He is giggling as if he is blowing the candles of a birthday cake. We are momentarily distracted by this as we want to make sure he does not burn his fingers.

I turn back to see Sharavana Baba's head flip backwards in his chair. His neck bent with his face looking upward to the ceiling. Sharavana Baba's breathing now changes into short sharp gasps as his body goes rigid and shakes. A servitor notices what's happening and enters the room in a fluster. He moves us away from the chair as Sharavana Baba, his whole body now quaking with tremors, slides to the floor. His body now writhes as he lies on the floor and moves along in a strange twisting motion.

As we are ushered out of the room, Jane has a

final glimpse of what's happening. "His body was writhing on the floor, and with my clairvoyant awareness, I saw him turn into an actual snake. He was Sharavana Baba but, at the same time, he was a snake! Craig and Danielle didn't see this, but this is what I 'saw'.

From Danielle's viewpoint, she said later that Sharavana Baba appeared to have smoke coming out of his mouth. From her sceptical mindset, she wonders out loud if he's been smoking the drug called spice!

The Interview

No sooner had we been ushered out than we were called straight back into the room. Sharavana Baba was now lying on the floor with his left hand in a large bowl of turmeric powder. We are told by the servitor to each take some from his hand. Sharavana Baba is still in a trance.

We step out of the room again and put the turmeric into some tinfoil that someone brings from the kitchen. We wait a few minutes and return to the room. Sharavana Baba looks momentarily tired from what has happened but snaps back into his normal jolly self. I am seated next to him, and a servitor joins us to help with any translation.

"You have many helpers on the other side. Especially your grandfather and father," he says as if nothing untoward has happened and was now aware of the spirit world.

"That's because my work in life is as a medium," I reply. The servitor explains what I mean by the word 'medium'.

"From the age of 64 swami will be important to you," continues Sharavana Baba.

"I am 64 now," I say. "The Naadi says I will meet a guru who is younger than me at this age. You're not older than 64 are you?" I joke.

Sharavana Baba is in his 30's. He laughs, his eyes twinkle, and he rubs his bald head. It is refreshing to talk with a guru who can laugh with you and even add a little self-deprecating humour like this.

On another level, what he was saying may be referencing something that others have mentioned before. Sharavana Baba once said, "Do not come to me or be with me with the expectation of better days to come." This has been interpreted as meaning that once the seeker has met the Sadhguru, the good days have already arrived. There is no need for expectation. Tomorrow has become today. It's time to live in the present moment.

It seems that our meeting was predetermined. Those who have read my other books will know how I am in awe of the Naadi predictions. I later checked my transcripts that predicted my meeting a special spiritual advisor at around the age of 64. The Brahma Naadi for example, says: "This gentle person will get a special blessed spiritual advisor, not at first will he let him know about his ways. This child here will have to find out about his whereabouts for himself and who he is. When the time is ready, he will know."

It strikes me that this could refer to Sharavana Baba though the Naadis also say that there will be other masters in my life too. "He will have interest and knowledge of several spiritual beings and masters, and he will take from them freely what he feels is in accordance with his inner understanding and knowledge." This insight may explain why I am not the devotional type. When I have the great good fortune of meeting enlightened teachers, my inclination is not to grovel but to approach them as I would one of my best friends. I often worry that this is an egotistical stance, but with Sharavana Baba, it certainly feels that you are sitting with a good friend—and in this instance, a good friend to the whole family.

Sharavana Baba with Damian

Only moments ago, Sharavana Baba had been writhing around like a snake, and now we were sitting talking about our spiritual lives as if nothing had happened. One of the servitors offers to take a photograph of us all together with Sharavana Baba. The man struggled with my phone camera, and Damian bounced back and forth, making it impossible to get a clear shot.

"Five thousand years ago, Agastya saw this moment in the Naadi," I say. Sharavana Baba looks at me with a mischievous smile on his face, and we simultaneously say, "And we can't capture a single instant of time!" We are in fits of giggles, yet surprisingly the photo came out just right.

"Okay, you two break it up," says Jane. "You've been talking to him for ages. Now it's my turn. You got anything for me?" I move out of the way. Jane sits next to Sharavana Baba.

"Why didn't you come to Kerala as I asked you to do last time?" says Sharavana Baba in a gentle tone.

"I've been looking after my mother."

"Yes, it is good to look after your mother. This is good." Then his eyes light up, and he beams at Jane and says, "Well, if you don't come to swami. Then I guess swami had better come to you!"

The shock on Jane's face was quite a picture, and mine must have been the same. My mind whirled through my packed calendar—we'd never be able to do that. I gave Jane my don't-ask-me-it's-up-to-you look.

"Before I return to India, I will come to your house and give Dharshan to your family and people you know," continued Sharavana Baba. "You have a nice room?"

"Yes, I have a nice Spiritual room," replied Jane.

"Yes, I know with lots of prayers there. But you also have a big cream coloured room and two cats," he said as if knowing the complete layout of our house. "We can use this one. What dates can we do?"

Jane and I started exchanging dates and wondering how we could juggle things. "When I come to you, I will reveal something very important. You will understand it later," he says. "You will understand it on the day."

We found it funny as he had simply invited himself even though it would be hugely complicated. There was only one date possible: immediately after we returned from our holiday in Barcelona and the day after our granddaughter's birthday treat to see Harry Potter Land. We were going to be exhausted and very pressed for time. Jane and I were worried about how we could possibly organize an event at such short notice. We could do a few things like sending out invitations before we fly, but we'd have next to no time to sort everything out on our return.

"Don't worry, swami will look after everything", reassures Sharavana Baba, perhaps seeing the shock on our faces and maybe also the whirlwind of our thoughts.

As we were leaving the room, it crossed my mind that I'd also written a note to Sathya Sai Baba asking that Damian could be cured of Diabetes. It was a tall order to ask for an incurable illness to be lifted. Yet after asking for help, along came the Naadi oracle with advice that had brought us here to this holy man who, some say, can cure all sorts of things. Would all this really work?

As we stepped out of the door, Sharavana Baba held up both hands in blessing. He smiles and says, "Sai Ram'.

We got back home quickly and missed all of the bad weather and traffic jams. We were just in time for Danielle to feed Damian properly, sort out his insulin and take Damian's sister, Willow, to Brownies, where she was looking forward to getting her new badge.

All this was quite a culture shock for Danielle.

We'd thrown her in at the deep end again, and she still wasn't sure about it all. I have to admit; it is a little odd—taking her to see a happy, holy man who also writhes around like a snake.

CHAPTER 9

Barcelona

We had a couple of days to prepare things before flying to Barcelona for a vacation, but there was so much more to do.

"We must find a caterer," said Jane as we boarded the aeroplane for Barcelona. "We need someone who can do the right sort of vegetarian food. We'll need a special chair for him to sit on. I'll need to buy a new dress, fresh flowers, fruit, candles, lights, a puja table, some new plates, a side table, a basket for people's shoes, the garden will need to look good, a footstool, signs, so people know where to go, do some invitations, …"

"And that's not all," I replied. "I've received an email about what's required when Sharavana Baba visits a home."

I showed her the list.

"Banana leaves!" she gulped. "Where on earth will we get banana leaves? And what's a 'Guru Peedham?"

she asks as she begins to read the room-by-room list of requirements. "His seat must be covered in brand new cloth…" she reads. "And what's a kumbam, and where will we get one? And where will we get beetle nut leaves, vibhutti, sandalwood paste and red kumkum powder—whatever that is!"

It was a comprehensive list of mysterious things impossible to source. Jane would also have to do an Arathi using camphor on a bed of holy ash, and we'd need to ensure that the 'Om Sharavana Baba Arathi chant' was played at this time. We must also supply soaked coconuts and a large knife to break them, plus a silver tumbler filled with water and camphor. A prasadam offering must be available made from a home-cooked food such as Pongal. (I thought that was a festival in Thailand?) We also need flower garlands, traditional ethnic Indian clothes, a ghee oil lamp, ghee a kumbam lamp, a tray of sugar candy, a coconut pot and a large silver tray.

"And there's more," I said. "It says here in the email that the house, cupboards and fridges must be cleared of non-vegetarian foods. And quote: 'Ladies of the household and ladies attending must be clear of their monthly menstrual cycle by at least a minimum of 7 days.'"

I was beginning to find it funny. "Would you like to tell everyone or shall announce it?"

It was clear that Harry Potter had nothing on the magic tricks that we'd have to pull off. At least dragon's teeth were not on the list. Actually, they'd probably be easier to source—we could likely get those at the Harry Potter gift shop.

Superhuman Shopping

Fortunately, Jane had already done a frantic shop at TK Maxx before we flew and had bought the guru seat and other furniture requirements as well as bought some glittery lights and cloth floor coverings. Jane has superhuman shopping skills—she teaches other women how to shop. She can spot a bargain at a thousand paces and will walk towards discounts at a gait that I find hard to match. Her mind will process a memorized shopping list like a quantum computer plugged into CERN. Uber shopping is a rare gift that, on this occasion, I was grateful she had mastered.

We could source the flowers, fruit and normal stuff from Sainsbury's—Jane already had all that in her radar—but all the Indian ceremonial trappings were going to be more challenging to find as there is no Indian community or Indian shops in or near our hometown.

"I'm going to try to forget it all for a week," said Jane as the aeroplane's wheels screeched on the tarmac of Barcelona Airport. "Let's just relax and enjoy our break. Sharavana Baba had said not to worry and leave it all to him. It will happen as it's meant to. I'm sure we'll sort it all out."

We'd have one day before Harry Potter and a day after that, so maybe it was possible? I agreed with Jane. We'd now have to just go with the flow.

Barcelona and Snake Gods

Barcelona is a beautiful city. We'd always avoided Spain ever since we'd had a vacation in Benidorm that we took many years ago when Danielle was little. It was the only place we could afford at the time, and we stayed at the same hotel as they filmed the farcical 'Benidorm' TV series from 2007 till 2018.

The nightclub at our hotel hosted the 'Sticky Vicky Show' in which a stripper did death-defying tricks with a razor blade. I had terrible memories of Benidorm and painted all of Spain with the same brush. I remember that when we arrived there was a drunk lying unconscious on the reception floor. In the swimming pool, drunks were doing backstroke as they drank beer from glass bottles. The Bingo caller had dyslexia. In his thick Spanish accent, he'd call out things such as "Knock at the door; Forty Two and One and Two; twenty-one," so you just didn't know where you were.

It was paradise for most Benidorm tourists, but it wasn't quite the inexpensive holiday in the sun that we were hoping for. The worst thing about the hotel—and Benidorm as a whole—was their insistence on playing the song 'Hey Margarita' by the dreaded Los del Río in every restaurant, bar event and shopping mall. It was like a subtle brainwashing technique to spread some weird propaganda. The song became my nemesis.

A few years later, when Jane and I went to Puttaparthi in India to see Sathya Sai Baba, we ate at an Indian restaurant in Bangalore. This was our first meal ever in India. The host looked like Mr Bean and insisted on picking his nose as he served the food. Instead of heartwarming sitar music, the restaurant blared out the song 'Hey Margarita'. It seemed so funny and incongruous. In fact, we took it as a Lila— a cosmic joke in the divine play. Maybe East and

West are not quite so different.

But I digress. Barcelona is not Benidorm. It is a wonderful city, crammed with culture, fantastic food and genial people. Jane and I were keen to see the holy sites of Barcelona, such as the nearby Montserrat Monastery. Our first stop was the Basílica of the Sagrada Familia, where we could sit in the cool of the cathedral and reflect upon what had happened and what was ahead.

"So what was all the snake business that Sharavana Baba did when he writhed on the floor?" asked Jane as we sat in the interior of the cathedral and watched the incredible dance of coloured lights from the spectacular glass windows designed by Antoni Gaudi.

"I felt I knew what was happening. I feel that I've seen it before in a past incarnation," continued Jane. "I could tell he's gone into a snake. I tried what he did when I got home. I tried sitting in a chair and wriggling my body to the floor. It really is so painful to do. But to slide down so gracefully and then wriggle your body along the floor is impossible. When he touched the Turmeric, it looked as if his hand had become a real snake. And then all the Turmeric came out the mouth. To me, it's like a healing snake."

"Like a caduceus," I replied.

"Yes, a healing snake," said Jane.

I had done a little research and had spoken to my friend Vivek, so I explained that this is what they call the 'Naga Baba' and seeing it is called the 'Naga Darshan'. Vivek had explained that this happens only on a Tuesday and that it is very rare for even close devotees to see this.

The Naga Devathas are the snake gods of Hinduism that are half-human and half cobra. The

Naga are said to be powerful and handsome. They can take either a wholly human or wholly serpentine form. Like a snake, they can be dangerous but are usually considered to be beneficial to humans.

In Hinduism, the heavenly worlds are divided into fourteen different realms called the lokas. The Naga live in the subterranean netherworld of the universe called Naga-loka, or Patala-loka. The lokas are grouped in three sections called the Svarga (the upper regions), the Prithvi (the earth region) and Patala (the underworlds). Patala has seven lokas.

Now, a Christian may freak out on hearing all of this. 'Underworlds' and 'snake people' inevitably bring to mind satanic forces. It was the snake that tempted Eve but also brought with it knowledge. (Why did God create the snake if he didn't want us to taste the apple of knowledge?) In the Christian imagination, one could easily envisage cuddly Sharavana Baba writhing on the floor and spitting green slime at the ceiling, just as we saw in the film *The Exorcist*. I have to admit that it is hard for most westerners to accept all of this. It's hard for Christians and harder still for atheists.

Hindu cosmology describes the Naga netherworld as a place filled with glorious palaces, beautifully bedecked with gold and precious gems. It was to this place that the Hindu creator god Brahma relegated the nagas. This was not as a form of damnation but because they had become too numerous on earth. He commanded them to bite only the evilest souls or those destined to die prematurely. In some ways, they are similar to the dragons of western mysticism or the protector deities of Buddhism. Just like the dragon, the Naga can be the guardians of treasure. Similarly, the snake is the life force that must be awakened in kundalini yoga and the perfectly balanced, snake entwined healing staffs Asclepius and Hermes.

From a psychological perspective, this could also be described as an archetypal symbol. Carl Gustav Jung writes in his book, *Man and His Symbols* about the serpent: "This is the universal quality of the animal as a symbol of transcendence. These creatures, figuratively coming from the depths of the ancient Earth Mother, are symbolic denizens of the collective unconscious. They bring into the field of consciousness a special chthonic (underworld) message."

In my opinion, Sharavana Baba was not demonstrating some psychological, figurative or symbolic act but was making a real connection with the heavenly worlds—the lokas. I read that on the far eastern side of his ashram in Kerala is sited a beautiful temple dedicated to the Sri Naga deities Sri Rahu and Sri Kethu.

In Vedic astrology, Rahu and Ketu are known as two invisible planets, and references to these two influences, in the form of planets, has also been part of my own Naadi readings that I have cited in my other books.

CHAPTER 10

The Naga/Sarpa Loka

The word Loka in Sanskrit means world. We live now on the earthly plane and above and below this plane exist other levels that are themselves divided into many more levels. Although we can exist in these other planes in a disembodied state (when in the subtle and causal body for example), it is perhaps wrong to explain them as afterlife planes such as heavens and hells.

Hindu cosmology tells us that creation is an endless phenomenon. It is unfathomable and ultimately as incomprehensible as the Divinity itself. Creation is God's play (leela) and is impossible for even the gods to measure. Perhaps lokas are like the physics theory of the multiverse—a hypothetical group of multiple separate universes, including the universe in which humans live.

Our karma determines which lokas we enter when

we die and how long we are able to stay. When the karma holding us to a loka is exhausted, we take earthly birth again. Now, just as a medium can connect with our loved ones in the afterlife, so too our consciousness can penetrate the multiverse. Could it be that this interstellar consciousness may also connect with other intelligent life forms? I have not heard Sharavana Baba talk about this directly, but I feel that he is in contact with the spirits and gods and the Nagas that legends say were once the teachers of mankind.

In his mind-boggling book *"Apprenticed to a Himalayan Master",* Sri M (Madhukarnath) describes an encounter with the Naga in the Arundhati cave near Rishikesh. (I describe my own visit to these caves in my previous book *"Messages from the Universe".*)

He was with his guru Maheshwarnath Babaji when a large snake appeared out of a two-foot-wide fireball. It was hooded like a cobra and was glowing in an electric blue light as if made of glass with electric filaments inside. To Sri M's relief, the cobra touched the feet of his guru Maheshwarnath Babaji who introduced the snake to Sri M as Nagaraj, the deputy chief of the Sarpa Loka. The snake had 'intelligent sparkling eyes' and touched Sri M's head with his forked tongue.

After the snake returned into the fireball and disappeared, Maheshwarnath Babaji explained to Sri M about the Naga:

"In the Milky Way, there exists a stellar system with seven planets and eighteen moons. One of these planets is called *Sarpa Loka*, and is entirely inhabited by highly evolved, hooded snakes…. Thousands of years ago, when humanity was still in infant stages of mental evolution, there was regular contact with *Sarpa Loka*. The wise and evolved Nagas frequented the earth and spent long periods here, teaching and educating human beings. The snake worship you come across in the ancient civilizations is a tribute to the advanced Nagas of yore."

Maheshwarnath Babaji tells how Patanjali—who wrote the *Ashtanga Yoga Sutras* and is often depicted as being half man half snake—was one of these Nagas. The snakes we see on the pharaoh's head and entwined around Shiva are symbolic of the ancient knowledge given to certain human beings.

Continuing this bizarre but fascinating story, Maheshwarnath Babaji says that humans became corrupt, felt threatened by the intellectually and spiritually superior Nagas and used the powers that they had learned against them. A war ensued, leading to the massacre of most of the Nagas, with the rest returning to *Sarpa Loka*. A few were left behind on earth but, through millennia of inbreeding, became retarded and no longer possessed the powers of their ancestors. The serpents and snakes that exist today are their ancestors.

The snake is one of the oldest and most widespread mythological symbols. Snakes represent healing, evil, fertility, rebirth, the phallus, the umbilical cord that connects us to Mother Earth, and so much more. Did something happen long ago at the dawn of human consciousness that still echoes in our archaic memories? Could it be that we were once in touch with a higher order of knowledge that only a few highly conscious people today can connect with?

The legends say that some of the Naga are still

living and guiding us. Some say that they take the form of snakes by way of self-protection, as humans are afraid of snakes. The further you dig into our ancient origins, the stranger things become.

At Sharavana Baba's ashram, the Sri Naga Temple shrine is considered to be the most sacred and powerful aspect of the ashram. Every Tuesday, an elaborate special Pooja is performed here to Sri Radhu and Sri Kethu.

According to Sharavana Baba, Sri Radhu and Sri Kethu are critical for the development of our life. This includes family development, the development of wisdom and of good health. When we witnessed the 'Naga Darshan', we were drawing upon the benevolent healing of the Naga, which was exactly what the writers of the Naadi must have hoped for Damian.

I explained some of the above to Jane as we sat beneath the vaulting roofs of Antoni Gaudi's masterpiece at the Sagrada Família. Jane had been taught by Catholic nuns as a child so had had a lot of fire and damnation teachings thrust upon her from an early age.

"I 'saw' him as a snake in my mind's eye," she said. "So I feel it's true that he was in contact with some higher dimension. And I'm sure Damian will benefit. I'm also sure Sharavana's visit to us will all fall into place. He said not to worry. Apart from all the Indian stuff, it's the food that's the biggest problem. I can't be cooking AND doing all the rest. You'll have to get us some caterers."

We sat in silence for a while and looked around at the magnificent interior. The Sagrada Família truly is a beautiful holy place and a suitable spot to reflect upon spiritual things. Gaudi designed the beautiful architecture here to express Christian belief. Each of the 18 organic-looking towers has a special significance. The middle represents Jesus Christ, and around it is four towers representing the Gospels.

Every detail says something about the Christian message. But it is Gaudi's harmonious use of light that most expresses divinity. The walls and pillars are plain and so become the incandescent screen for the kaleidoscopic play of coloured light. The rainbows of colour accentuate the plasticity of the building and are naturally conducive to introspection.

I pondered how the world's many religions are like a stained glass window, and the one clear light breaks into many colours expressing the same divinity in many forms. Jane and I had just been talking about Hindu concepts that, for some, may seem to be contra to Christianity, but, indeed, are not all religions basically the same? All believe in one omnipresent God of love that speaks to us through the language of the heart.

It is good that different faiths exist as there are many people in the world, and all have different temperaments and cultural influences. However, we must respect the differences in the many faiths and see them all as valid. It is the one clear light—the One God—that shines through them all.

My phone went ping to tell me a text message had just arrived. "Oh, that's a bit of a coincidence," I say to Jane. "It's Vivek. He asks if he can come to the event at our house for Sharavana Baba's darshan. And can he bring his mum too?

"He says they will bring the food. They will bring a

rice dish or daal for about 20 people. It will be vegetarian and suitable for this sort of event. So it looks like that's sorted, and all I'll need to do is supervise the washing up and hoovering."

"Our house has certainly seen some strange things," chuckled Jane as we arrived home and stepped into the hall. "We had our wedding reception here with a booming, lederhosen-clad German Oompa Band playing in a garden marquee. I've given birth in a water birthing pool in the dining room. We've held séances here and spoken to the dead for so many people. We've had Korean film crews storm through the house; the BBC make a TV series here, News Night broadcast from the garage and all the rest. We've had famous people visit—friends of Princess Diana visit. Pop stars visit. Royalty visit. And now we have a holy man, coming all the way from India, dropping in!"

Despite our misgivings, we managed to get everything organized in two days—even the banana leaves. Jane was worn out. She felt it was like having the Dalai Lama or a king visiting the house.

"I think my house must have been in shock," she says. "We were told that when Sharavana comes, he *may* go upstairs, to your bedroom, and he *may* open drawers and cupboards. It's been known for him to look in drawers and pull out things. In one case, he rooted around in a drawer, took out a picture of Mother Theresa and told the homeowner to put it on display so that its energy could radiate. If he goes upstairs and all my piles of ironing fall on top of him, it will be truly blessed."

Fortunately, Sharavana Baba devotees told us—at

the 11th hour—that they would be able to bring the things we couldn't source, such as the sandalwood paste, kumkum powder and so on. But there was still masses of work to do. For example, Jane spent many hours removing the thorns from all of the roses that Sharavana Baba was to hand to people. Meanwhile, I made the flower garlands to put around his neck. A quotation from a florist told us they would cost between £300 and £400 to make at short notice so I went on YouTube and worked out how to do it ourselves.

I must congratulate myself on the quality of my fine artistry. It took me a long time, and lots of needle jabbed fingers, but I finally managed to make a magnificent garland of white and deep magenta roses intertwined with other carefully selected flowers. It is self-evident that I really am a clever person when I want to be. I have an excellent eye for detail, proportion and colour. I tried it over my own head and knew it would be a perfect fit. Jane was also pleased to see her 'man that never does anything in the house' at last do a useful domestic task.

I called the Sharavana devotees to let them know what we had done and that we were nearly ready to receive swami. "Oh dear, you mustn't try on the garland. This will pollute the energy. Only Swamiji must wear it," said the voice through the telephone. "But don't worry, we can pick up a garland for you from the Indian shop."

It had been a frantic two days, but now everything was in place. As a final touch, Jane placed a beautiful unworn sari over the new chair that was to be used by Sharavana. She'd bought the pure silk red sari some years ago just down the road from the 'Hey Margarita' restaurant in Bangalore on our way to see Sathya Sai Baba in Puttaparthi. At the time, I'd moaned because she'd spent all of her spending money on it—this was a wedding sari that families save for years to buy. I was right when I told her that it was a wild shopping frenzy whim and she'd never wear it (I always say that) but wrong in saying that it would never come in handy.

We put the cats in the cattery so that they could not mess up the display. Our home was now a full-size version of the Alhambra Palace—slightly better actually—and we could safely leave it all in place and go to see *Harry Potter*. We could enjoy a day of birthday wizardry with our grandchildren and the next day greet a holy man at home.

CHAPTER 11

Who is Sharavana Baba?

Sharavana Baba was born on 11th October 1979 to a low-income family in the Indian village of Sreekrishnapuram of the Palakkad district in Kerala. He is the eighth child in the family of nine children. His birth name is Sri Murali Krishna Swamiji though he is now known by his spiritual name Sri Sharavana Baba.

The village of Sreekrishnapuram sits in a green tropical area near the Kunthipuzha river, which is one of the tributaries of the river Thuthapuzha that flows through the Silent Valley National Park. It's a poor area, but I would imagine—despite the poverty—a beautiful place in which to grow up.

Sharavana Baba is said to have exhibited signs of

divinity from the start. His website claims that he was born self-realized and fully aware of his divinity. Devotees tend to "over-egg the cake" a bit, but it does appear that he exhibited signs of divinity from his early years.

It is claimed that snakes were sometimes found in his cradle. This idea, of course, would horrify western mothers, but to the Hindu, it is a sign of divinity. In particular, the cobra is one of the many symbols of Shiva. It is also said that a cobra appeared under the cradle of Sathya Sai Baba when he was a newborn baby. In fact, there are many other similarities in his life and sayings that are strikingly similar to the story of Sathya Sai Baba, which I will mention later.

In Sharavana Baba's case, his mother returned and saw that her son was playing with snakes. They were licking his face. The child was giggling and loving every moment. Naturally, his mother was horrified, and she chased them away, but they were to return many times, which led the family to believe that their son was very special, perhaps even divine.

As a child, his demeanour was one of saintliness. He was always absorbed in prayers and helping others. He went to the local village school and was 'a role model for other students. He enjoyed cooking food for the students. When he left school, he worked as a hotel errand boy and later as a porter for the local butcher, carrying sacks of meat on his head and delivering them to restaurants.

Throughout his teenage years, he regularly visited temples and prayed. His wages were scarcely enough to feed him, so sometimes he begged and used the proceeds to give to others. He suffered many privations in his early childhood and teenage years and worked very hard to maintain his large family.

Gradually, people began to notice that here was a young man who worked very hard but also had an extraordinary spiritual remit. People also invited him to their homes to perform devotional ceremonies and prayers and sought his advice and blessings. His followers grew in number, and eventually, Sharavana Baba went public with his mission. He held public prayer meetings and addressed large audiences in several towns and cities in India.

His mission gained fuel when his uncle helped him by relocating him to Trichy, where he was given a job in a lodge as 'Waterboy' serving water to the guests. The Lodge owner and his wife liked the boy, who was very popular with the guests and decided to support him. Sharavana Baba was also given a small pooja room in the corner of the Hotel where he began his spiritual work. In particular, he was helped by the lodge owner's wife, who recognized the boy's calling and helped him start his mission, which gradually grew immensely.

Today Sharavana Baba is looked to as a Sadhguru, which means a living self-realized master. An Enlighted being, you could say—an expression of the Supreme Self in human form. Indeed, many now flock to him for solace and many claim that he has changed their lives. Some seek refuge at his feet, anticipating that he will support their souls and clear the negative effects of their past karmas. The Sadhguru gladly bears the karmas of his devotees and helps them to quicken their spiritual advancement. Sharavana Baba explains that although we may think we have visited him in the hope of receiving blessings, the reality is that he pulls us to his presence.

This was certainly the feeling we had when we first met him in Fareham and now when he casually invited himself to our house. As the mafia say, 'it's an offer that you cannot refuse!'

Sharavana at our home

East Vs West

From what I have seen, most of Sharavana Baba's devotees are from an Indian background. The homes we visited and the public events were geared towards Indian pageants and tradition. There are comparatively few white faces at the time of writing this (2018), though I am sure that this will soon change. Sharavana Baba visits the UK, Europe and Canada, but his audiences are primarily from the ethnic Indian population. In Hinduism, the guru is seen as God in human form and is given the utmost respect. Westerners, however, are quick to criticize and question the wisdom and knowledge of a guru.

My worry with gurus of all kinds is that once the western ways take hold, the energy changes. Just as westerners have turned hatha yoga into a farcical circus, so too these delicate flowers of eastern mysticism can be turned to plastic. It is apparent that Sharavana Baba is trying to raise a lot of money for his spiritual projects. As I have explained, he builds ashrams, temples, schools, feeds people, and runs many welfare projects.

Naturally, one worries if this could turn into another Bhagwan Shree Rajneesh (Osho) who, through his weird gun-toting cult, amassed a mind-boggling wealth of 100 million dollars, bought up the town of Antelope in the USA and had 93 Rolls Royce cars. In this age of Kali Yuga, it is hard to find true gurus as darkness has shadowed their world, too, and modern times have seen many examples of spiritual degeneracy.

The same problem also befalls the Naadi Shastra. They were designed in a time when palm leaf readings and remedies were given for free. Today the intention of many Naadi readers has changed from a pure one of free service to a mercenary one. This is why, in most cases, the power of the Naadi to foresee the future and offer remedies has been lost. If the reader becomes corrupt, the Naadi loses its power. Consequently, I consulted multiple Naadis with different readers and looked for similarities in the messages. In my case, I was fortunate to find several readers whom I believe, to be honest. Sadly, most others fail to see a genuine reader.

I'm pleased to say that Sharavana Baba appears to have very few detractors. A case was brought against his trust on the 24th March 2011, claiming he is a 'fake swami interested only in amassing wealth' but, if you read the details, it all appears to comprise very flimsy accusations. Nonetheless, I expect in due course that someone else will "take a pop" at him. Spiritual people always attract enemies who want to undermine their good work. I've seen it in my own life and, in particular, was horrified by how many attacked the avatar Sathya Sai Baba.

As a rule, the problems often lie not with the gurus but with the devotees. If you look to a guru in order to escape responsibility or for a quick fix to your problems, then you are on a slippery slope to nowhere. People chase after gurus in order to overcome their difficulties or are simply curious, or because they hope to lose their notions of emptiness and purposelessness. Some love the feeling of self-importance that comes from being a guru follower. Their egos seek the guru's attention and approval. Others become dependent on the guru, which weakens their own nature.

The true purpose of a guru is to be the bringer of light. Therefore, we should look to a guru to achieve liberation from the ignorance of our own darkness. In my opinion, this should not mean giving up our spirit of self-dependency and self-determination. Our primary relationship is always with the infinite—what many call God. The gurus are the messengers of the omniscient and omnipresent God.

When a brilliant light like Sharavana Baba walks through the world, there will also be shadows from which detractors will emerge. There are many tricksters and fraudsters, of course, but when faced with the impossibility of the truly miraculous, there has to be an escape exit for those who can see no further than the objective model of reality. I have known this with the wonders of mediumship, with the miracles of Sathya Sai Baba and the marvels of the Naadi Shastra. I'm sure that, as Sharavana Baba's powers flower, many will want to counter his light and challenge him.

Guru Worship

In India, Hindu children are generally brought up to respect holy men and women, and a devotional attitude comes easy to them. They call this devotional attitude Bhakti. Bhakti is a Sanskrit word that literally means 'attachment, participation, fondness for, homage, faith, love, devotion, worship, piety'. It is most commonly understood as devotion to God or a person who is believed to be an embodiment of God, such as an enlightened person. In the Bhagavad Gita, it is given as one of the possible paths of spirituality and takes you to moksha (salvation).

I have never felt inclined to grovel. Perhaps my ego is just too big, or maybe because I feel that God does not want us to be beggars. I like to think that I come into this life as a student but must leave it as a teacher. Realizing our divine nature is our birthright as we are all God already but just don't know it yet.

When I say that I am not the devotional type, that does not mean that I don't respect spiritual teachers. In my book and film *'Mystic Journey to India'* I meet the aesthetic Siddha yogi Maha Ananda Siddha who lives in a cave and can sleep in a fire pit. I am in awe of men like this who can forgo their material wealth and undergo extreme privations in order to fulfil their spiritual tasks. Similarly, when Jane and I went to see

Sathya Sai Baba in Puttaparthi, I had no inclination to start crying or begging for guidance. I saw a spectacular figure, but I also saw the same friend who would appear in my dreams and make jokes. Same, too, with the female guru Amma. When she hugged Jane and me and giggled, I felt that we were in the arms of someone from our own family.

In the western world—and to an extent now in modern India—rationalism has replaced spirituality and intuition. Because of this, we have become intellectually lopsided. Our inner world is fossilized because our intellect is not underpinned by spiritual intuition, making it dry and destructive. Too much rationalization, intelligence and over-thinking deepens delusion and starves wisdom. Cleverly reasoned ideas will endure for a time and be popular and topical, but the great ideas of the spirit endure forever because they are founded on direct soul wisdom revealed by intuition and supported by reason. This is something that modern people need to rediscover.

What I like about Sadhguru Sri Sharavana Baba is that he is approachable, fun and human. When you meet him, it's like meeting someone you've always known but have somehow forgotten. It's like meeting a best friend from school where the conversation takes off as if you were talking only yesterday and no time has passed. This is how Jane and I felt when we first met Sharavana Baba—we were all best mates.

I have described the man Sharavana Baba, but anyone who meets him soon realizes that he also functions on another level of consciousness. His inexhaustible energy and ever-present cheerfulness can be achieved only when he has merged his consciousness with the higher reality. Jane and I can joke with him, yet we feel him working with us on a high spiritual level. Our mundane minds communicate, but so do our souls as they chuckle their way to awakening.

Sharavana Baba is a realized being who is enjoying the bliss of spiritual advancement. He comes in an approachable human form to share his joy and, most importantly, to help us realize our own divine bliss. From what I see and from talking to his followers, he does not want to amass wealth, gain fame, or be worshipped by millions. He is not happy when people throw themselves at his feet. He simply wants to share with us the ineffable bliss of higher consciousness and discover that we, too, have the same ever-blissful, living divinity within us.

CHAPTER 12

The Sathya Sai Link

Many people who have come to Sharavana Baba were previously devotees of Sathya Sai Baba. If you are familiar with the teachings of Sathya Sai Baba, you will note many similarities in Sharavana Baba's discourses at the end of this book. In turn, if you read the discourses of Sathya Sai Baba, you will note many similarities in his work with the teachings of Vivekananda, Mahavatar Babaji, Swami Sivananda Saraswati, Anandamayi Ma, Ramalinga Swamigal and so on. This is because all of these great men and women speak directly from the source, from the font of eternal truth, from the ancient yet ever-new knowledge called the Sanatana dharma.

For us, it often appeared that Sathya Sai Baba and Sharavana Baba were working with us in tandem. Not long before we'd visited the London ashram with our grandchild Damian, a friend in India had posted us a photo of Sathya Sai Baba and some Vibhuti ash. It arrived a few days after Damian was diagnosed with Type 1 Diabetes, yet the sender had no idea about our worries. On the back of the photograph—that showed Sathya Sai Baba materializing a lingam—was written:

"Sai Baba manifested the Golden Lingam during a discourse to college students at Whitefield, near Bangalore, South India. Many people have been healed by touching this photo to their bodies. An Indian medical doctor, Dr Doraisingham, from London, England, raised a child from the dead by holding the photo against his body. Sai Baba says that wherever this photo is kept, there will be blessings, healings and miracles."

Our Indian friend had also included the Gayatri Mantra, which, you will remember, was the same mantra given in the Naadi reading and also chanted by Sharavana Baba when he held my grandchild Damian. It was reassuring to know that so many powerful energies were driving things forward.

Others have said that they feel there is a correlation between the energy of Sathya Sai Baba and Sharavana Baba. There are accounts on the web of how a UK home visit by Sharavana Baba in April 2011 saw "sacred ash pouring profusely from the statue of Sri Sathya Sai Baba, the huge photograph of Baba, the idol of Shirdi Baba and a host of other divinities aligned along the shelves of the sitting room."

When we were making the final preparations for Sharavana Baba visit to our home, I was preparing the puja area in my yoga room and stumbled upon a Sai Baba dream I had written down on a scrap of paper.

It was dated seven years ago. I had dreamed of Sathya Sai Baba arriving at our front door, but he looked like somebody else when I looked at his face. In the dream, I am asking myself, "Is this Prema Baba?".

Moments before reading this dream, Jane had commented and said, "Doing all this detailed preparation is like having Jesus or Sai Baba coming to visit us."

My dream about Sai Baba also contained a sequence in which He is speaking to me. I asked him to write it down for me so that I could remember it in the real world. I am very excited at the prospect of physically transporting something from a dream into real life.

Sai Baba writes on long strips of yellow paper. It is in a strange script, and I am amazed to see how tiny his writing is. I can make out a few words in the minute text that says "Samastha Lokah Sukhino Bhavanthu," which is a Hindu prayer that translates as "Let all the beings in all the worlds be happy." Sai Baba had changed the wording slightly from the traditional mantra to refer to *all* the worlds—not just this physical world.

Sathya Sai Baba then looks at me and says, "Learn to die more slowly."

"Does this mean I am going to die soon?" I reply. (Those who have read my book *'Messages from the Universe'* will remember I had a similar dream set in Varanasi).

"No," replied Sathya Sai Baba, "but other people will find this piece of paper hard to interpret."

Later in the dream, I hand the yellow paper to my friend and yoga teacher who can read some Sanskrit. "I think it means to give up your astrology preoccupations," he says.

"No, you are wrong," I reply.

I sat on the floor by the puja area of my yoga room and marvelled at what I was reading. I could remember the dream now. I recalled how the dream had puzzled me for ages, but now it made sense just hours before Sharavana Baba was to visit our house. The long yellow paper strips with the infinitesimally tiny writing are Naadi leaves of course. The Naadi palm leaves are yellow, and the ancient Tamil writing is written in a very tiny shorthand script so that huge amounts of information can be recorded on a single leaf.

'Learning to die more slowly' was one of the core messages of the leaves as, through the remedies, I had extended my life. The first consultation had said I would die at 75 years old, but in later consultations, the leaves said that I would now die at the age of 85. My mantras to the mother goddess Shakti given to me by the earlier Naadis from different readers had extended my life by 10 years and maybe more.

The dream had occurred three years before I had made my first Naadi consultation. Clearly, Sathya Sai Baba was predicting that his message to me was to be found on the leaves, but I had no idea what he was showing me. The impossible had happened. I really had brought something from the dream state into physical reality.

I sat and pondered the significance—if any—of stumbling upon this dream at this auspicious time before the visit of a Sadhguru. Could Sharavana Baba also be the rebirth of Sathya Sai Baba, who knocked on my front door in this dream? Sharavana had been born before the death of Sathya Sai Baba so this was clearly not the case, but I felt that both of these great souls were connected and came from the same source.

I'm jumping ahead a little here, but when Sharavana Baba walked near the spot in our house where I had read the note, he chanted the unusual version of the mantra from my dream: "Samastha Lokah Sukhino Bhavanthu". (Most Hindus would have chanted the traditional rendition of the mantra Lokah Samastha Sukhino Bhavantu)

I've talked to other followers of Sharavana Baba, and many say that they see the face of Sathya Sai Baba on Sharavana Baba's face. Others say that Sharavana Baba has revealed himself to them as Mahavatar Babaji, the miraculous saint described by Paramahansa Yogananda. And some say that he is the rebirth of the jivanmukta Ramana Maharshi.

For newcomers to Indian ideas, all these Babas and so on must get very confusing. The fact is that Sharavana Baba appears to be connecting to us from a very high place. In essence, he is at one with the divine source, just as all these other masters were. At heart, they are all the same, and they are all part of the One just as we, too, are all part of that same One. When you meet a high spiritual master, God speaks to God through God, for God is everywhere.

CHAPTER 13

Coming Home

"He's here! He's here!" shouted Danielle excitedly from the upstairs bedroom where she was giving Damian his insulin injections away from the crowd of guests sitting on the floor in our lounge and conservatory. "He's in a black car, and it has the number 666 in the number plate!"

Everyone was alive with the buzz of excitement at the prospect of a holy man visiting our street. Neighbours were leaning out of their windows to see what all the parked cars and fuss was about. If you didn't know what was going on, you'd be somewhat surprised to see a fancy car and brightly coloured holy man step into our middle-class bourgeois cul-de-sac.

I could see from my vantage point that the nosiest of them all was standing behind his curtains and had his binoculars out again. He is exceptionally competitive and wants to spread all the gossip. In the past, he was so desperate to know why we had a TV crew visiting our house that he knocked on our door to ask us what was going on.

"Don't you know?" answered Jane with an incredulous look. "It's the BBC News. We won the lottery. Sorry, I can't explain it all now as we are about to broadcast live."

We left him with that thought for a number of days. In fact, we were filming a TV series called *'Our Psychic Family'*. Goodness only knows what he thought today's commotion was about.

Maybe Jane can tell him it's a visit from the Dalai Lama or a President from Africa.

Many of our neighbours were sitting quietly on our front room floor, patiently awaiting the guru. We hadn't sent out invitations but just let it all happen. We wanted people to be guided by providence. If anyone asked, they could come. We told our family about the visit, and a few close friends and anyone our intuition told us to ask, but, for the most part, word spread by its own accord. In the end, we had a few famous people, some family, some neighbours, some people from the Indian community and others who arrived through fortuitous circumstances. Everyone sitting there was spiritual seekers and would benefit in their unique way. Everything had fallen into place.

As the car arrived, I went out to greet Sharavana Baba and placed a flower garland over his head. He then stepped into the front hall where Jane did an Aarti puja in front of him next to the kumbam. This is a vessel filled with water on which a coconut is placed and adorned with five mango or beetle nut leaves and a flower on top. The coconut is decorated with vibhuthi ash, sandalwood paste and red kumkum powder. Next to it we placed a tray of sugary candy. Somehow we'd managed to source everything we needed.

The Aarti puja is done on a silver plate with light from wicks soaked in ghee, a flower and incense. It is a symbol of removing darkness but also can be an expression of many things, including love, benevolence, gratitude and prayers.

"All the time, I was hoping I wouldn't drop it on him," said Jane when I spoke to her about it all afterwards. "It was the first time I'd done something like this, and I was worried I'd set his robes on fire! I'm sure he knew my concerns because he smiled broadly and said, 'Are you happy?' No truer word" laughs Jane. "To be honest, I was very happy as it would all soon be over, and I could relax!"

When Jane had finished, Sharavana Baba took the rose petals from a bowl, threw them over us and blessed everyone taking part. He then walked to Jane's spiritual room to the left of the hallway. This room is where Jane does her spiritual work and gives her psychic readings. It is filled with colourful images of Lakshmi, Padre Pio, Sai Baba, spirit drawings by Carol Polge, gold Buddhas, statues, crystals, Chinese furniture, crystal balls, and an Aladdin's Cave of spiritual stuff. Sharavana Baba smiled and blessed the room and said, "Very good energy. Very good energy."

He then walked through the lounge with all the neighbours chanting 'Om'—you don't see that often—and through my library and office and into my spiritual room where I do meditation, yoga, naadi remedies and puja. We were followed in by Danielle, Domenico and our grandson Damian.

"Domenico, my future son-in-law, is an atheist," said Jane when describing the event. "He looked in shock when Sharavana Baba touched his arm and said 'very strong' which is so true—he is a very supportive person and is like a rock to Danielle and their family."

He then handed Jane a coconut, and a flame appeared. He told her to pray. "I was praying for all the children of the world and for Damian to be helped," recounts Jane. "Just as I finished my prayer, the flame went out. I took this as a good sign." Sharavana Baba then broke the coconut with a large knife.

He turned to Danielle and said, "Don't worry. I have come here to help Damian." He looked at Domenico and repeated, "No fears. You are very strong." He then looked at me and said, "Very happy. You have done very well."

Sharavana Baba then started chanting mantras, walked through the house and sat in the chair in the area where everyone was assembled. A lady from his party then made an introductory talk about her first encounters with Sharavana Baba and how it changed her life. As with so many other followers, he appeared to know everything about her and her family and knew about all her personal problems and concerns. He knew the date of her wedding anniversary, for example, and how she had holy water from Lourdes hidden in her drawer at home.

She explained that there were a great many things said that he couldn't possibly know. He also made predictions about her future that came to pass exactly, and how she had seen many people cured of an illness by him, including cancers, brain tumours and how the doctors couldn't explain how the scans now showed fully healthy people.

One thing from the talk that stuck in my mind was that Sharavana Baba told her that "You never seek the guru. The guru seeks you." This seemed to be very significant for Jane and me, too, for it felt to us that Sharavana Baba had effortlessly entered our lives. We were not seeking solace or desperate for help when we first met him. Our lives were in harmony and our minds at peace. It was as if the time was simply right for a new spiritual influence to take part in our lives and help us to climb a little higher. The teacher came uninvited. And we were happy that it was so.

Another devotee (Pavan) explained in a talk about the meaning and purpose of having a guru. He explained that the guru takes us from darkness to light and helps us realize our own divinity. We can seek God in ourselves and in other people too. He explained how Sharavana Baba's discourses often talk about eliminating ego and finding the purity within yourself. Sometimes he instructs people to chant mantras that protect a person from harm, but the ultimate goal of the path is Salvation—for the soul to rest in God. The guru helps you achieve this goal and enables you to deal with your life and see through problems in your day-to-day life. The mantras can help you to overcome troubles.

In particular, he explained how Sharavana Baba teaches the Subramanya Asthostram Mantra—the 108 Names of God. God has many names, but there is divinity everywhere. You should pray to the aspect of God that you are most comfortable. For example,

Sharavana Baba says—as did Sathya Sai Baba—that if you are a Christian, you should strive to be a good Christian.

I sat ready to record the anticipated talk by Sharavana Baba when he looked at me and said, "Now you give a talk. Tell them about Swami and the Naadi." I was unprepared for this but spoke about some of the ideas of Hinduism and the story of how the Naadi Shastra had triggered a series of events that had led to this event's happening today.

Unfortunately, because of my unexpected call to give a talk, I was unable to reach the button to record Sharavana Baba's discourse. I don't want to paraphrase it here as it would lose its authenticity, but I will include some of his recorded talks at the end of this book to give you a taster of his philosophy.

I noticed that there were tears in a few people's eyes as he spoke. Sharavana Baba spoke simply about how we should help one another. He also talked about our past life actions and how these have brought everyone together today, and how the actions of our ancestors make it possible for us all to be here together now. We must be thankful for the efforts and sacrifices of our ancestors.

Towards the end of his talk, Sharavana Baba said that life originated on Mars. He didn't elaborate, and I wasn't sure if he had said that it was life—i.e. cellular life—or our earliest ancestors who had come from Mars.

Mars is important generally to Sharavana Baba's teaching as it is the ruling planet for the Indian god Murugan (Lord Subramanya.) In Vedic astrology, Mars is called Mangala or Kuja and is the son of the Earth and is a focus of energy or shakti of the Earth.

Mention of Mars and of our originating on Mars also had significance to me personally. I have noticed that when I give an inspired address at Spiritualist churches, the spirit world sometimes drops in specific and personal messages to the people sitting listening. They may have come to the church with a question in their minds, and woven into my address comes the answer. This is something that we mediums know happens but are unconscious of its happening at the time.

Mars was important and was a sort of confirmation about something I was researching. At about this time, I was helping my friend Sri Saktibaanee with his new book about the Jeeva Naadi called *Sukham Tharum Sundra Kandam*. Sri Saktibaanee had asked me to write the foreword and prepare it for print. The book had been revealed through the Jeeva Naadi and was a direct communication from the Tamil Saint Agastya.

Usually, to consult the Naadi Shastra, we use the thumbprint to find the palm leaf with its predictions. However, the Jeeva Naadi is a blank leaf, and the words appear directly on the leaf as light and disappear again after the reading. It is a miraculous communication with the great Rishis of the past—a palm leaf telephone that leaps through time. (A similar thing happens with the miraculous Pothis from Andra Pradesh.)

The Jeeva Naadi is extremely rare, and there are many fakes out there, particularly on the Internet. Sri Saktibaanee, however, had been researching the Naadi and Pothis for a large part of his adult life and had stumbled upon a genuine Jeeva Naadi.

The reader was Hanumathan Dasan, the custodian

of the Agastya Jeeva Naadi and Bogar Jeeva Naadi. One day, while he was waiting for his next client, the leaves began writing messages directly from Maha Guru Agastya. The most important part of the messages was to offer a way to overcome the corruption of some of the Naadi readers. To stop the extortionate charges being made for Naadi remedies and rituals, Agastya gives a set of simple remedies that anyone can use to eradicate the negative effects of past karma. Anyone can do these at no cost.

In short, the communications tell us to read and re-read specific passages in the fifth book of the Ramayana of Valmiki. The messages tell us which parts to read and when to read them. Sometimes there is a little astrology involved, too, but the method gives us a simple way to overcome just about every problem and obstacle that a person may encounter in life.

I was intrigued by the fact that Agastya was saying, here, that the Ramayana is much more than a book of holy stories. It is also a magical treatise that can wipe away misery.

I am in awe of the lost knowledge of India. Today, we have left just a fraction of the record of a time in prehistory when people could perform superhuman feats using some higher form of consciousness. My earlier discussion about the serpents of the Naga Loka also points to these times when humankind was in touch with higher intelligence—perhaps from another order of reality.

When Sharavana Baba spoke about life originating from Mars, my brain lit up, for, when I look at the Ramayana, it appears to me to be a mythical story of a time when we may have been in touch with advanced beings. It is tempting to think of the gods like Hanuman as extraterrestrials and the army of monkeys as early humans.

Sharavana Baba did not say any of the above, but I wonder if he has somehow tapped into my thoughts. In many of India's holy books and epics are references to technology such as flying machines and weapons that are the stuff of science fiction. The Mahabharata describes divine lighting and laser weapons, and a weapon that can hypnotize.

In the Ramayana, there is a description of flying machines called Vimanas. These could navigate to a great height with the aid of quicksilver and a massive propulsive wind. The text also describes a beautiful chariot that 'arrived shining, a wonderful divine car that sped through the air'. Elsewhere a chariot is seen 'sailing overhead like a moon.' To me, these things sound reminiscent of aeroplanes and perhaps even spacecraft. And how would you explain this passage that reads "The Puspaka car that resembles the Sun and belongs to my brother was brought by the powerful Ravan; that aerial and excellent car going everywhere at will… that car resembling a bright cloud in the sky.".. and the King [Rama] got in, and the excellent car at the command of the Raghira, rose up into the higher atmosphere."

I have digressed, of course. It is, nonetheless, fascinating to read these ancient texts and know that they are more than myths. The Agastya Jeeva Naadi tells us that our very nature is subtly transformed by simply reading the Ramayana. Perhaps this will inspire you to read some of these fascinating and spiritually uplifting classics of India.

Meanwhile, back at suburbia, Sharavana Baba had finished his talk and would now give a one-to-one interview with everyone in the room. While I tucked into the delicious food brought by Vivek's mum, our guests could now have a short talk with swami.

Sharavana at our home

For many of the people in the room, this was their first-ever encounter with spiritual India. Sharavana has a charming manner that immediately makes a person feel at ease as if they are in the company of someone they have known a long time. I have never seen him frown. He seems to know the main problems in a person's life and, in the few minutes people sit with him, he will get straight to the heart of the issues that are troubling them and sometimes even reveal things that may become important later. Jane and I were able to ask some of the guests their reactions.

For our friend Caz, he appeared to know that she had a battle with illness. "He looked straight in my eyes and told me that I had health problems," says

Caz. "No one would have guessed as I looked perfectly fit but had recently been diagnosed with a serious condition. Sharavana pointed two fingers to his open eyes and told me not to worry. 'I will be watching over you,' he said. He gave me some Vibhuti ash that I have been taking regularly, and I feel my condition has improved.

"I found Sharavana Baba a very gentle, caring and compassionate soul, full of empathy, a knowing man who can reach into each of our core beings and can reach into our inner thoughts and sift these out, letting us know that he is very much aware of what is going on and why. He made me feel secure, a unique individual, not just a mother, wife, friend, colleague, but ME: someone that needs love and attention, not to be taken for granted or used."

Some of the neighbours we'd invited were sceptical at first but were shocked when he revealed things about them. "He gave me the rose," says our neighbour Tina. "He then said, 'A rose. Just like your name.' But how on earth did he know my middle name was Rose!"

Similarly, he seemed to know all about our neighbour Tony. "How's your mother," he asked her as she sat down. He handed her a small packet of blessed turmeric. "Give this to your mother. She's a very good mother. And you are also such a good driver." All this was also very significant. Tony's mother had a bad heart, but his comments about being a good driver had a personal significance to Tony. For another couple, he was immediately aware that they were teachers and had been made redundant. "Do not fear; you will get work," he said. My friend Frank was bewitched by him. "I couldn't believe what happened," said Frank excitedly. "He kissed me on the head and gave me a gold coin."

Every person who spoke with him was told something uniquely significant that applied to them and no one else in the room. Present was our friend and the well-known television presenter Melinda Messenger who felt her encounter was spiritually meaningful. "Being in the presence of Sharavana Baba left me with an unforgettable feeling of 'wellness;' there is a simplicity and gentleness in his manner and presence," says Melinda. "Our meeting has left a lasting impact on me, and I hope to spend some time at his Ashram in the near future."

The most fascinating comment came from Vivek who, you will remember, introduced me to the Naadi Shastra and later to Jane and my first encounter with Sharavana Baba. "I had a dream that Sharavana materialized a ring on my little finger," says Vivek. "When I had an interview, he held my little finger and said, 'How's your little finger?' Every time I meet him, I am amazed by how much he knows about me."

Sharavana Baba had been with us for over three hours, and now it was time for him to leave. We were tired, but Sharavana Baba never seemed to tire. At public events, I've seen him give interviews with people all day and into the late evening. Some of his close devotees tell me that they all feel energized when they are with him but flop after he leaves. I've noticed this too. When we've sat with him, our energy soars but drops again when all is finished.

As we walked towards the front door, he put his head to mine and rubbed my head with affection.

"Very holy man," he said. Then he turned to Jane and said, "Happy?"

"Very Happy," replied Jane. He giggles and says, "Very holy woman."

As he stepped out of the door, someone came and put the silver sandals on his feet. They were beautiful with lotus flowers on them. He glanced towards the woods opposite, "Good energy here. Good energy."

He walked towards his car, opened the glove compartment and handed Jane some liquorice and sesame seed sweets.

"Are they free?' joked Jane. He laughed and said, "Yes."

"I'll have one then," replied Jane.

Sharavana Baba handed her the sweets, put both thumbs up and beamed like a child. It is such fun to banter and joke with him, and yet, behind all this play, we are all aware that there is a deep spiritual dimension to all that is happening. It's heartening to be with people who understand that spirituality can be fun.

As the car disappeared down the road, Jane looked at me and said, "I like him. He's fun. And I feel he likes us too because we understand who he is but also enjoy his human form. I've seen bliss in his face today and transfiguration in his face when we were in London. I'm sure there are things about him that are beyond our comprehension. It's like meeting an old friend.

"I'm convinced we knew him from a past life. We all played together in a village. I can remember us all throwing stones. We didn't have a lot. We were all throwing stones some time long, long ago in ancient India."

CHAPTER 14

Rameshwaram

The energy in the house seemed to remain high for a long time afterwards. People often comment about the powerful aura our house has, but people seemed to be wowed by it during that period. A music teacher friend of Jane's, who missed Sharavana Baba, arrived late but wanted simply to sit in the energy still resonating through the room.

It all sounds a bit New Age Californian, but we could all really feel something. On the day we'd had Muslims, Hindus, Christians, and Spiritualists all sitting together and sharing spiritual peace. If your heart is open, you'll feel it. Whatever your faith, the energy of the divine is the same for all.

I believe the energy also continues to resonate with Damian. The Naadi reading and its warning had triggered this whole series of events. We had seen the holy man that it had foreseen, but there were still other remedies to be completed before the work was complete.

My next step was to get in touch with my friend Mr Prakash in Tamil Nadu, India. He is a Naadi reader who helped me with some of my readings but chaperoned me through India when I went there to do my remedies and make my movie *'Mystic Journey to India'*.

Although Mr Prakash had not been the one to consult the Agastya Naadi, I would commission him to do the remaining remedies by proxy. The remedies can sometimes be very expensive, so, as a matter of course, I will always give the remedies to a different Naadi reader from the one who gives the reading. This is a safeguard against corruption and stops Naadi readers from making false predictions and adding expensive extra remedies. If they do not get commissioned for remedies, there is less chance of expensive extras being slipped in.

Damian's remedies were quite expensive as several priests had to be hired for many very long pujas. I'd made some enquiries about having them done in the London temples, but they were reasonably complicated pujas to be done at different times and would have involved a lot of travel. Although it is best if Damian, or I as his representative, were to sit in, I opted, in the end, to have them done by proxy in India. I trusted Mr Prakash as we had become friends while I was in India and remained friends afterwards.

Most of the puja and homa remedies were done in Rameshwaram at the Ramanathaswamy Temple. This fascinating and incredibly beautiful temple complex completely blew me away when I went there to do my own remedies by having a dip in the sea followed by 22 baths from the holy wells. It's believed that all your sins are washed away and health regained after the bathing from all these wells. My own experience of this place was spiritually overwhelming. I knew that Mr Prakash would connect with it in the same way I had. God is omnipresent so whatever happens at the Ramanathaswamy Temple simultaneously happens to Damian and the rest of us back in Hampshire, England.

Fortunately, Mr Prakash already had plans to visit Rameshwaram so we didn't have the expenses of flights across India. He also organized the priests and videoed all the rituals. Again, to prove it all had been done and to make a connection with Damian, an A4 photograph of him and his family is placed in the temple setting as the pujas are performed.

The Naadi also told me to give a gold coin to a 'monk or Brahmin as per the choice of the blood relative asking to hear about this boy.' For this one, I arranged for a gold coin to be given to Maha Ananda Siddha, who told me incredible things about my future the last time I'd been to India. Maha Ananda is the 19th Siddha in the lineage of the famous Maha Siddhas of South India. He lives in a cave and exhibits miraculous powers such as sleeping in a fire pit and never eating. He is a master of Siddha Medicine. I describe my encounter with him in my book of the film *Mystic Journey to India*.

In addition, the remedies included 125,000 chants of the Gayatri mantra, which, in total, took eight months. We were also instructed to feed beggars and monthly feeding of a school for disabled and mentally subnormal children. On top of this was car hire, hotels and a fee for Mr Prakash.

So did Damian get better?

Damian still has Type 1 diabetes, but there have been some noticeable changes. Previously, he'd been having convulsions and was frequently being rushed into intensive care. Damian still has to have injections before he eats anything, and there are still great dangers associated with even the most common illnesses.

His parents, Danielle and Domenico, continue to have their work cut out in being the 'human pancreas' but things have most definitely improved. Now, Damian has a *Dexcom Continuous Glucose Monitoring System* plugged into him all the time, which means that the parents are alerted as soon as the sugar levels become unstable.

We are not claiming a miracle, but it was extraordinary how suddenly the hospital services improved. Previously, there seemed to be no help, lots of gaffs and endless delays at getting proper treatment. Previously, Domenico was red in the face trying to get the right help and right equipment from the NHS. Now things are going smoothly, and I'm convinced that Damian will live an expected lifespan.

The Naadi had said "If he gets the blessings of a guru as soon as possible, there is no danger to his life." The Naadi also predicts that once the obstacles are overcome, he will go on to live a happy life, marry and between the ages of 41-45 will go on a pilgrimage and meet a sadhu/guru who will shower blessings on him.

I believe that the encounter with Sharavana Baba and the Naadi remedies have countered the adverse effects of his past life karma, and Damian will live a long and normal life. I trust in the incredible clairvoyance of the Naadi seers who have conquered time and have foreseen our fates in the present time. It was they who 'saw' that a blessing from Sharavana Baba is the spiritual catalyst that would set the course of providence.

The ancient Naadi seers were attuned to the oneness of creation. They realized that God (Divine consciousness or whatever you prefer to call it.) is in the past, present and future, in every action we take and every thought and feeling we have.

The mysterious power of the divine runs in all that is material and all that is non-material. The divine exists both in time and beyond time. It springs from within us and from without us. God is in all. Be happy, for God is everywhere.

PART 2
Be Happy

CHAPTER 15

India Calls

In the search for spiritual truth, the seeker occasionally hits a seam of gold. These moments are determined by the planets' positions, by our past life karma or sheer good luck. Who knows? Today was one of those golden seams. Not only were we to meet Sharavana Baba, but we would meet up with some spiritual friends who had many beautiful stories to share.

As you know by now, Jane and I are psychic mediums. I make some of my income by giving clairvoyant and mediumistic readings by telephone. Clients call me from all over the world to ask questions about their lives or communicate with their loved ones in the spirit world. The work is inspiring, exhausting and challenging. The readings often reveal extraordinary back-stories, open empathic connections and sometimes trigger friendships with the people who call.

One of my regular callers is Desirée and her husband Andrew from Switzerland. I had promised Desirée that if she were to visit London, we could meet up. She enjoyed my work as a medium but was also keen to meet my wife, Jane, who she knew is also a well-known medium.

Desirée and Andrew – and others in their family - had a series of readings with me. One of the first spirit messages I gave Desirée was from her grandmother in spirit, who spoke about her disabled son Dan. She said that Dan had a form of autism caused by lead poisoning. Similar messages came through when I made a connection with her mother in spirit. She talked at length about Dan and his troubles and what they should do to get him into the right school. I felt very connected with Desirée and her family because of the similarities she had to our grandchild Damian's struggles.

Many spirit communications came through during this series of readings. The most poignant and evidential spirit message was from her first husband. I knew from the impressions he was giving me from the spirit that he was Italian. When a medium 'hears' a spirit voice, we hear it in our mind in our language. This spirit contact is a mind-to-mind communication, so I would hear his voice as English even if the spirit did not speak English during earthly life. I was able to tell Desirée that her first husband was a very kind and intelligent man. I said he was a nuclear physicist. Despite his scientific training, he had been open to the fact that there was life after death.

The spirit showed me that he had died in distressing circumstances. I could feel myself in a confined space and gasping for breath. Then it suddenly became clear to me.

"He had a heart attack during a flight to Germany," I said. "I feel he wants you to know that he is okay now and safe in the spirit world. He is talking about terribly confused circumstances afterwards. At the time of his death, he was desperate to get a message to you. He says that you know what he is talking about."

Desirée understood. At the time of her first husband's death, nobody called her to let her know what had happened. She waited for his arranged call at 6:00 pm, but nothing came through. She called the airport, called the airline, called the hotel, called his work, and the police called everybody, but nobody was authorised, willing or able to tell her what had happened. Only when she finally reached Interpol could she learn what had happened.

It is hard to imagine the desperation she must have felt, knowing that something terrible had happened to someone you love far away from home. Two months later, to add insult to injury, the police came to her to let her know that her husband had died.

"Thank you, but I have already buried my husband," she said to the police.

Connecting to Sharavana

It was during one of these consultations that I told Desirée about Sharavana Baba. I mentioned the extraordinary presence and healing energy that Sadhguru Sharavana Baba appeared to have. "He's visiting London soon," I said. "Perhaps he can help you with your fifteen-year-old son Dan."

"You sent people to me from Switzerland," said Sharavana Baba when Jane and I next visited him.

How did he know that? It turns out Desirée and her family checked Sharavana Baba's itinerary from his website, saw he was soon to visit London, so they immediately booked a flight to meet him. Desirée, her husband Andrew and her children, were inspired to meet Sharavana. They loved his energy and his loving manner. Dan didn't want to leave. Sharavana's draw is magnetic, and Dan doesn't want to leave.

"Have no fear, this boy will be all right by the age of 21," Sharavana had said at their first meeting. "He is not an ordinary child. He is like me."

Dan's disability inhibits him in many ways, and yet he is also brilliant. He has deficits in communication, emotion recognition and expression and social interaction but has no intellectual disability. Sometimes children like him have extraordinary talents that are an incongruous contrast to their overall handicap. In Dan's case, he appears to have extrasensory perception abilities – what the yogis call Siddhis.

In Dan's case, he knows the layout of places that he has never visited. Desirée told me how they had taken him to hotels abroad, and he'll know the exact location of all the toilets and facilities immediately. He'll also know how to get around cities he's never visited and even has detailed knowledge of the bus routes. All this without having any previous access to this information.

One of the most astonishing instances was when he said that they must take the number 10 tram to their destination. The person accompanying Dan told him that this was incorrect as the number 10 only goes to the airport. They must take the number 11 tram. Dan repeated to her and insisted that it would be the number 10 tram. The next tram to arrive was number 10 with an apology from the driver who explained that the number 11 had broken down. He had been diverted to pick up the passengers for the number 11 tram.

On another occasion, Desirée's oldest daughter rang her to say that she'd just seen Dan at their house. She was in a fluster as this was so strange since Dan and his father had left the house some time ago to spend the afternoon in the nearby park. Could he perhaps have the power of bi-location?

Dan seems to have the ability to intuit information. In some tests, he scores 100% even though he has never studied the subject so, in many ways, he is just like Sharavana, who likewise knows many things instantly and without study or access to information. Sharavana Baba dropped out of school as a young boy and had very little formal education, and yet today he is very knowledgeable on most subjects. He has a wealth of knowledge about Indian spirituality, Sanscrit and the stories and teachings of the Vedas that fill his discourses. Like Dan, he seems to draw his information from an invisible source, consistently 100% accurate. Extraordinary people enter a state of wisdom that is higher than the knowledge obtained by reasoning and inference. Perhaps this is what Sharavana means when he says Dan is 'just like me'.

Healing Journey

I had also helped Desirée find her Brahma Naadi leaves with a reader who I trusted. The leaves revealed Desirée's name, birthdate and all the names of people in her immediate family. It also detailed the causes of her troubles in this life. It told us that Desirée lived as a holy man on Mount Kailash in Tibet in a previous birth. During this period, she upset a Siddha yogi who placed a curse on her. This curse brought much of the distress and health issues in this present life.

The Naadi also had a chapter that gave various remedies to lift this curse. We had the rituals and mantras performed in India by the temple priests at Rameswaram and arranged for several charitable acts done on her behalf. All this would clear her path and, in turn, help Dan forward.

It was with all this behind us we met for the first time face-to-face in London. Desirée had arranged a private consultation with Sharavana Baba and what better way to all get to know one another than to share the experience. It was exciting to meet at last and particularly under such auspicious circumstances as we sipped tea and waited for our turns to see Sharavana.

Desirée and Andrew had scoured the world to find a 'cure' for their son's condition. They told Jane and me the extraordinary story of their trip to Mongolia to seek a shaman healer.

"I'd come across a book which documented a family's extraordinary journey," said Desirée. "It was about a family with a severely autistic child who decided to seek the help of a miraculous shaman healer who lived in the wilderness that is the Mongolian-Siberian steppes. I was so inspired by what I read that I tracked down the author, and with his help, worked out how to get there. I then bought flights to Mongolia via China and arranged transport and guides to get Dan and the family to the tents where the nomads lived."

It was quite an adventure for her family that included five-year-old Dan, his twin sister Nicole and nine-year-old sister Isabella. After a full day of various shamanic rituals near the capital, the real adventure began, with four days of travelling through the road-less steppes of Mongolia, sleeping in tents. As they neared the borders of Siberia, the roads got progressively worse, and the last stretch of travel took place on horseback and – reindeer!

Finally, they reached their goal – the base camp of Ghoste, one of the foremost shamans in Mongolia. During three days of meetings and several ceremonies, Ghoste assured them that Dan would have no issues by his late teens. Intriguingly, Ghoste took a particular liking to Dan, said that Dan would be a shaman, and hinted he would like to adopt him!

It's hard to imagine taking a young family to such an extraordinary place.

"But that was not the end of it," continued Desirée. "We decided to invite a young Mongolian shaman back to the apartment that we had in New York. The problem was that it was hard to get rid of him. He decided that he'd be better off living under the dining room table, where he would sit and play his drums into the early hours of the morning. It was hard explaining to visitors why we had a man living under the table and harder still explaining the drumming to the neighbours."

Soon it was time for us to see Sharavana. Andrew, Desirée and Dan went ahead of us and had their interview. You go and sit with him for this, and he will tell you a few things about what's happening in your life and advise you about your spiritual path.

"Very happy to see you again," said Sharavana as he patted Jane's hand as we sat with him. "Are you happy? Yes, very happy. You must both come to my ashram in India."

"I can't do that," replies Jane. "The journey would be too much for me as I have high blood pressure."

"That's okay," he replies. "You are a strong woman."

He then told us some personal things about our lives and family. I mentioned that I had been – as he knows - deeply involved with researching the Naadi Shastras.

"I AM the Naadi," he replies as his eyes twinkle and face bursts into a wide smile. I chuckle as well as he has said this before and keeps playing with this idea. Of course, the Naadi is not just the oracles that I have spoken about in my books but also refers to the spiritual energy through which the life force called 'prana' flows through our spiritual and physical bodies. It is 'the way'.

"Will you write me another book?" he asks. I hesitate a little.

"Just a little book." He indicates a little book using his thumb and index finger. "A little, little, tiny, tiny, tiny book…."

It was hilarious as he seemed to be asking how a small child would ask for sweets. It was hard to resist.

"Yes, of course, I will."

"And India?" he says. "You must come to India, and I will teach you. Come for Maha Shivaratri"

"That's fine with me," interjects Jane. "You can go. I have no problem if you'd like to go."

There was no way out. It looks like I will be going to India again to write another book. Resistance was futile, and indeed when I looked at my old Naadi readings later, it started in several places that I would go to India to write books about the Siddha yogis.

CHAPTER 16

Predictions

"Coronavirus set to become an epidemic," said the newscaster as I drove to the hotel at Gatwick. It was now early February 2020, and few people understood the likely effect and extent of damage that Covid19 would cause to the world. When you go on a spiritual journey, the inclination is to put fears aside and go with the flow of events. There is a sense of being protected despite any potential dangers.

A sense that 'all will be well' surrounded me as I set off to see Sahravana Baba and celebrate Maha Shivratri. Great spiritual beings look out for and protect their devotees, particularly when they are on a spiritual mission. It's a bit like in the film The Blues Brothers when everything goes well every time Elwood Blues, played by Dan Akroyd, says, 'We're on a mission from God.'

Nonetheless, I still take no chances. I get my vaccinations and take out travel insurance. I recall the time in 1998 when we went to visit Sathya Sai Baba in Puttaparthi, India. A young doctor was travelling with us, and she had decided to have no vaccinations, malaria tablets, or insurance. She was very devout and would trust entirely in the power of Sathya Sai Baba to protect her. She came down with a stomach illness, and it took years for her to recover fully. I'm sure God protects us, but we also have to do our bit too.

My daughter Danielle – the mother of our grandchild Damian - tried to talk me out of going. She was convinced that the virus was going to spread further than China, and she was, of course, apprehensive that Damian would get infected. The virus would be devastating for anyone with Type 1 diabetes. On the news, we saw how China was on red alert and had built the 25,000-square-metre (30,000 sq yd) Huoshenshan Hospital at Wuhan in a matter of days. It was disturbing news.

Virus Predicted

Foremost in my mind was the fact that in 2017 I had predicted a world pandemic on my YouTube channel. I said that the world would soon see a virus that would sweep the world. I could not give the exact date, but we needed to prepare and take precautions. The Sun newspaper interviewed me about my predictions. It quoted me saying that there will be a 'global flu epidemic linked to global terrorism.' It gave the headline: 'Prophet of Doom Psychic who predicted Brexit, Trump, and Nice forecasts a deadly flu epidemic.'

Worryingly my predictions implied that the virus was deliberately released, and I commented on

YouTube that the virus could result from a laboratory leak. It may even have been deliberate to put a lid on the protests from the Hong Kong umbrella movement. We will explore this later and how the Naadis also foresaw the pandemic and clues its origin.

Historically, my spiritual work was about being a medium and providing proof of life after death to the bereaved. However, for me, the Spiritualist philosophy was full of many flaws that I found spiritually unsatisfying. Most people wanted reassurance that they would get to heaven after they died and live there forever with all their limitations intact. They missed the fact that the soul's true destiny is to awaken and be at one with God and that this requires us to do a lot of work on ourselves.

My spiritual interests were now more focused on knowing the meaning and purpose of life and how we can change ourselves to become fully awakened beings in both this world and the next. The naadi had also triggered a fascination with the nature of time and its relationship to consciousness. I was interested in the idea that all things may be a form of what the philosopher Friedrich Nietzsche had dubbed 'eternal recurrence' – that we repeat our lives in millions of different ways across a multiverse of possibilities. The ideas that were also taken up by thinkers such as Pyotr Ouspenskii tell us that we should love our fate and see everything that happens in our lives, including suffering and loss, as good or necessary.

I do not necessarily agree with these nihilist ideas, but it was clear that time is not quite what it seems to be. The naadis had proven to me that the ancient rishis had seen my past, present and future. The future is 'seen' by people who have conquered time, and as the naadis had told me, I would be able to do the same.

The looming pandemic brought thoughts about the future of the world foremost in my mind. This trip to India would provide me with some essential inner space in which I could contemplate these big ideas, and perhaps Sharavana would help me in some way to gain further clarity, either directly or through his spiritual influence.

The Call of Shiva

Destiny must have decreed that I would make this journey for the naadi had foreseen it: 'The native has to chant mantras and worship Lord Shiva. By doing this, the native slowly takes his steps towards maturity and to get Gnanam (knowledge). The native will get blessings from a guru born in a country far away from the native's country. The guru will be much younger than the native. The guru will be a Hindu and a person who will be worshipping Lord Shiva.'

Sharavana Baba was born in the village of Sreekrishnapuram in Kerala on 8 October 1979. He is 25 years younger than me, and he indeed would be worshipping Lord Shiva as my trip to the ashram was for the Maha Shivaratri celebrations. His spiritual name relates to the mantra 'Om Sharavana Bhavaya Namaha', which literally means 'One borne in the arrow-shaped forest grass' as Lord Murugan (Subramanya) was. The full meaning is 'Salutations to the son of Shiva, who brings auspiciousness and who is chief of the celestial army.'

So the naadi got it right. It is eerie how it foresaw my connection with Sharavana Baba in the above quote and subsequent naadi readings from different sources and readers. Occasionally, I will suggest some of my clients who come for clairvoyant consultations to visit swami. Strangely enough, he'll always spot people I've sent to him and will repeat back to them the exact same words I have said to them in my reading. I suggested an Indian couple worried about a curse that they visit him as his energy would help alleviate their fears. He knew right away that I'd sent them along and said, "Craig is the match, and I am the candle," which I think is a lovely sentiment in that I can spark their interest in spirituality, but swami will light the way for the rest of their journey.

Making Psychic Predictions

In the period leading up to my departure for India, the coronavirus pandemic was a looming worry in the background of everyone's thoughts. My YouTube channel got many hits and lit up because of the correct psychic predictions I'd made about Donald Trump and world events. Now my subscribers and fans were pressing me to make more predictions. It wasn't easy being the 'New Nostradamus' as the Star Newspaper had dubbed me. What had started as a simple psychic experiment was now becoming the central theme of my clairvoyant work. And just before the coronavirus pandemic, everyone wanted to know about the Trump presidency and its consequences for the world.

Ever since I first watched Trump on the American TV series 'The Apprentice,' I became interested in the man. He was the personification of arrogance, yet his straight-talking, childlike observations gave him an air of honesty. This presidency was a bizarre situation where the views of a multi-billionaire rang true with the ordinary person. His simplistic solutions and brash attitude would resonate with the many people who were becoming tired of liberalism and showbiz platitudes.

The media dismissed him as a clown, but I immediately knew that – like it or not - this man would be president.

Naadis predict vlogging

Every year, I make psychic predictions on my website and regularly post these in September for the coming year. On 11th September 2015, I posted my predictions for 2016. A consultation with the Naadi around this time told me to 'use the media of light and sound and new technology to begin your spiritual teaching.' I interpreted this as meaning that I should publish my thoughts on YouTube, and so began my vlog that became very popular.

For me, this vlog was just an experiment. I pointed this out to visitors and explained that psychics are fallible. 'Let's see what I get right' was my attitude. My main interest is in mediumship, but making predictions was interesting to try, and it seemed that the naadi was pushing me to do it.

Jane and I had made psychic predictions in the past, of course. It's hard to avoid it as the newspapers love the dramatic headlines that psychic predictions can provide. In 1994 we had a TV spot for a year on Channel 4's'The Big Breakfast' in which we would predict next week's news today. The infamous Paula Yates, the wife of Bob Geldof, was the anchor for the show. As I have explained in my other books, it became a very successful show, and the pundits were shocked by how much we got right every week.

One of the national UK newspapers picked up my YouTube predictions and made them into headlines on their website. I posted my predictions every year on my site and highlighted in green the ones I got right with links to news articles. I also highlighted in red any predictions that I got wrong. Together with the dates of the YouTube videos, it was easy to see when I made the posts. At the time, I had a monthly column for a UK magazine called 'Fate and Fortune' and emailed my predictions to my editor to prove the dates I had made the predictions.

Some journalists had been following my site and realised that my 2015 predictions for 2016 were almost all correct. They published articles about how I had correctly predicted, amongst other things, that Brexit would happen and there would be a terrorist attack in Nice, France. I had also predicted that Donald Trump would become president.

Other British newspapers picked up on the stories and called me 'the Prophet of Doom,' 'The New Nostradamus', and other dubious accolades. Soon Reuters released the report, and many of the national papers and big-name websites were talking about my predictions. Even the Independent – a broadsheet - published favourable headlines. In its haughty tone, it said, 'Craig Hamilton-Parker has had an uncanny propensity to predict global events.'

A psychic getting a positive accolade from the broadsheets was unprecedented. Jane and I are much more used to getting a thoroughly good kicking from the press. There were reports in India, Russia,

Czechoslovakia, and all sorts of places you'd never expect to see my face. My vlog had gone viral.

I should have known that all this would happen as the naadi had spoken about it already in May 2014 when I'd had my first naadi reading that I wrote about in my book 'Messages from the Universe.' The naadi had said that I would give weekly and sometimes daily discourses to millions of people worldwide. I had assumed that this had meant travelling, but now I realised I was doing what it had predicted via YouTube.

The Unexplained

A few months before making the trip, I appeared on an American TV show called The Unexplained. This programme was a popular show hosted by William Shatner, who played Captain Kirk in the TV series Star Trek. I was the show's expert on Nostradamus, and we made a program about his predictions and, in particular, about prophecies that related to the potential assassination of Donald Trump.

Many 'experts' believed that Donald Trump's election as president of the United States heralds the end of the world. They claimed that the 16th-century seer foresaw it all in Century III, Quatrain 81, where he wrote, 'The great shameless, audacious bawler. He will be elected governor of the army: The boldness of his contention. The bridge is broken, the city faint from fear.'

Nostradamus theorists said that the 'shameless, audacious bawler' is a direct reference to Trump and his outspoken, unapologetic style of campaigning. 'Governor of the army' was being interpreted as the leader of the world's most powerful military country, the United States.

Other cited lines from Nostradamus include Century 1,40, in which it says, 'The false trumpet concealing madness will cause Byzantium to change its laws.' The word 'trumpet' jumps out, of course. Byzantium was the capital of the Eastern Roman Empire and was the entry point into Europe. The feeling was that this was a reference to Trump's ambition to build a wall against immigrants and refugees. Similarly, the word 'trumpet' is mentioned in Quatrain 50. It says, 'the Republic of the big city' will engage in costly military operations, ordered by the 'trumpet.' This has been interpreted as a costly war initiated by President Trump.

Nostradamus made many predictions that can – in retrospect – be interpreted as references to Donald Trump and modern times. The one that the show focused on indicated that Trump might be in danger of assassination.

In my YouTube predictions, I saw Trump becoming ill and forced to quit the presidency for a time. He would, however, continue his presidency. I marked this as wrong on the predictions list on my website, but then I saw that Nostradamus appears to say something that could relate to Trump. His predictions look like an assassination attempt.

In Century 1, Quatrain 57 Nostradamus says: 'The trumpet shakes with great discord. An agreement broken: lifting the face to heaven: the bloody mouth will swim with blood; the face anointed with milk and honey lies on the ground.'

Could the trumpet be Donald Trump? A face lifted to heaven with a bloody mouth swimming in blood looks as if he could have been shot. Was this a revenge attack because of a deal that went bad for someone? The revenge of a foreign power, perhaps? Israel is the Land of Milk and Honey. Perhaps Israel is somehow involved?

In my predictions, I say that Trump collapses with a perforated bowel or some other stomach condition. Nostradamus seems to go much further.

Donald Trump Prediction

I had predicted that Donald Trump would become president generated a lot of interest in my work as a psychic. Soon before my flight to India, I had also caused a stir because I had managed to track down the Naadi for Donald Trump that revealed his future and his previous life as a Brahmin. These intriguing revelations were very much on my mind during my stay in India, so I will digress a little to let you know about some of the things that the Naadi had to say. Most importantly, the Naadi shows how the time of Maha Shivaratri can have a powerful effect on our future lives.

I had managed to get Trump's prediction through a very reliable source – a friend and fellow Naadi enthusiast who I'd known for many years. In the past, he had found the naadi for the missing child Madeleine McCann and sent it to the police. Unfortunately, they ignored it and only now are we beginning to see the Naadi's prophecies unfold.

In the naadis I have described in my other books, the dried palm leaf – known as a Patra – is found by using a man's right thumbprint. Finding a real naadi for a person is very hard. Most Naadi readers are fakes, and even if amongst one in a thousand real ones, there is still a high chance that the leaf will not be found as many of them were destroyed. The leaf will only reveal itself when the time is right.

It was extraordinary to be able to find Trump's Naadi. The Bhrigu oracle uses a slightly different method to the naadis of Southern India that uses the thumbprint or length of a man's shadow at the time of the consultation to find the Patra. We used astrology and Trump's birthdate to find it in the Bhrigu.

The saint Bhrigu who wrote these leaves thousands of years ago, was known as Guru Maharaj, the King of Gurus. He was one of the seven great sages known as the Saptarshis. Bhrigu was the first compiler of predictive astrology and also the author of Bhrigu Samhita. The legends say that he is a Manasa Putra – the 'mind-born-son' of Brahma.

Knowing how hard it is to get the Patra, I knew that Donald Trump's prophecy was something that destiny wanted to reveal. It could help the world. Most importantly, I wanted to get the message to Donald Trump himself to benefit from spiritual guidance. If the United States president is swayed onto a spiritual path, then this has to help the whole world. I don't endorse Trump as so much of what he says and does is shocking, but if he could somehow read the naadi, it may bring the best out in him and thereby help everyone. With this in mind, I made a YouTube video about the revelations of the Bhrigu. I revealed some of the general statements but not the very personal stuff.

The Naadi and Bhrigu take a neutral stance. They make statements about choices made now and in the past and the consequences of making those choices. They present their prophecies in a practical, matter of fact way and are completely non-judgmental. The writing on the leaves will lay your life bare so that you can see why you have the life you have and how you can change it. Its goal is to help you overcome the negative effects of bad karma and guide you to live a happier and more spiritual life.

The Bhrigu prescribes remedies – called 'Upayas.' These eradicate the adverse effects of past life karma. The remedies will help with problems now and in the future. They may be complex or straightforward. Remedies may include visiting temples and holy places, feeding children or animals or chants and rituals to appease poorly positioned planets in the horoscope. In my case, I had to give a cow and a calf to a low-income family, visit temples and holy places in Southern India and do various sacrificial fire rituals called Homas.

I believe that the destiny shown in the naadi and Bhrigu is a potential. It only comes to pass if the remedies are done so that your true and most positive destiny can unfold. Some prophecies will happen without doing the remedies because karma must unfold in this life.

Donald Trump's predictions corresponded closely with what I had already predicted on my YouTube channel. At the time, he was facing impeachment, and the Bhrigu corrected predicted that he would not lose the presidency. Again this corresponded to the predictions I had been making using clairvoyance.

There was also a lot of very personal material in the naadi relating to Trump's relationship with his mother and things he had done in his life. Also, it spoke of his illnesses, covert activities, business deals, and sexual relationships. These secret matters are written there as proofs of things that only Donald Trump will know. The information is there to convince him of the truth of the naadi. Its objective is to help set him on a higher path by doing the prescribed remedies. Therefore, it is not right of me to divulge these things, so I will limit what I have to say and omit some highly personal, accusing, or contentious information.

The ancient dried palm leaves speak of Trump's astrology and the position and meaning of the planets in his horoscope. It says, 'Mars is in the rising sign Leo, so he will at times not be able to control himself due to anger and arrogance. He wants to be in absolute control, just like a ruler.'

This drive to power is amplified by his Sun, which is in the tenth house with Rahu. In Vedic Astrology, Rahu is the shadow of Saturn, whereas Ketu is the shadow of Mars. Rahu represents materialism, mischief, fear, dissatisfaction, obsession, and confusion. The oracle says that this means Donald Trump will 'seek by any means and desire the highest office possible.' Also, Jupiter, in his second house, 'will grant him wealth from birth, and he will inherit from his parents.' It also points out that Rahu is also influencing his second house, meaning that he will 'often speak rudely and not tell the truth.'

It is important to remember that this astrological interpretation was written centuries before Trump was born, yet the ancient seers anticipated the exact details of his horoscope. Rishi Bhrigu next looks at the '12th Lord Moon in Trump's 4th house,' which is weak and predicts that his mother 'will not be very happy in this lifetime.'

Psychoanalysts have suggested that Trump may not have bonded successfully with his mother. Some have argued that his sometimes strange behaviour may result from his childhood interactions with his mother. His mother, Mary Trump, became seriously ill during the labour with her last child and, after an emergency hysterectomy, had recurring infections and surgeries.

The psychoanalysts say that separation from the mother can create a compulsive need to be in the spotlight, attachment anxiety, and results in a drive to seek approval. Could it be that the young Trump's trauma of separation from his mother during this period moulded him as an adult and made him into the politician that he is?

Little is known about the actual emotional state of Mary Trump. It certainly must have been difficult being married to a powerful man like Fred Trump. Remember, she was born far away in a tiny pebbledash croft house owned by her father since 1895 in Tong on the Isle of Lewis, Scotland. Local historians have described properties in this community at the time as 'indescribably filthy' and characterised by 'human wretchedness.' Emigrating to New York at the age of 18 and marrying one of the most powerful men in America six years later must have been a problematic metamorphosis. It is reasonable to surmise that this new life could have made her unhappy and that the Naadi may be right in saying that his mother's unhappiness shaped Donald Trump's character.

This same position of the Moon in his horoscope will cause other problems. 'His mind will be full of desires, and he will go to any lengths to fulfil his desires and demands,' says the thousands of years old text. 'He will have all the wealth in the world but also a lot of secrets in regards to his properties, wealth, debts, women, and sex. He will gain huge wealth on account of properties, but also, there will be a lot of secrets and foul play to gain what he desires.'

His birth chart has Mercury in his 11th house but 8th from his debilitated Moon. This planet position means that 'he will be able to do a lot of business, real estate earnings, and gain a lot of money. However, he will also lose a lot, and he is not always telling the truth about how he has got what he has.'

More is revealed by his Venus and Saturn, which are in the 12th house. The Bhrigu Samhita says of this: 'This foretells that he will have many sex affairs, adultery, scandals and losses in life. He will have several foreign affairs too. His wives are mostly born in other countries. His health is not always the best, and he should be cautious about his temper, blood, heart, and venereal diseases.

There has been some press speculation about whether some of Trump's behaviour may result from syphilis. Dr Steven Beutler wrote an article titled "A Medical Theory for Donald Trump's Bizarre Behavior", published in the media organisation New Republic and claimed that Trump's irrational behaviour might be caused by untreated syphilis.

Trump and Maha Shivratri

Parts of the manuscript are a conversation between the Saptarishis sage Bhrigu and his son Shukra. Shukra asks what happened in Trump's previous life and the reason for his present life.

'Oh Shukra,' replies Bhrigu, 'In his former life, he was a priest in a Shiva temple. Every day, while doing his work, he was a drunkard; he was always telling lies and always cheating other people while doing the offers and prayers to the Lord. On Shivaratri day, a king came to the temple to offer pooja at the Shiva lingam. He offered a gold pot to Lord Shiva.

'But this man, after some days, took and sold the gold pot to buy poisoned liquor. While very drunk, he attempted to do pooja to Lord Shiva in the temple. Such destructive and ominous deeds will follow him also to this present birth, and he will even pursue to enrich himself similarly if need be in this current birth.

'To help him overcome such bad deeds, he is advised to do pooja to Lord Shiva every day. And on Maha Shivaratri once a year, do the Rudra Abishekam and also the Kalasarpa Pooja. Otherwise, there is a risk that he may fall from the highest office to the lowest status completely humiliated.'

Trump and India

Donald Trump has projected himself as an uber-wealthy playboy, yet he is a proud teetotaller. He says he has never had a drink, smoked cigarettes or consumed drugs. Trump told reporters that his abstinence from alcohol was 'one of my only good traits', and yet the Bhrigu Samhita identifies this as his greatest weakness in his past life. Perhaps he learned a lesson.

The sage continues by saying that Trump has the potential to regain the spiritual level that he had before alcohol destroyed his status in his former life. I was very interested in watching how Trump responded to President Modi when he made the Namaste Trump inaugural tour of India on 24th and 25th February 2020, and just after I had returned to the UK.

An attendance of over 100,000 applauding people was a positive message to counter the impeachment problems back in the US, but it did also seem that Trump was genuinely enjoying India. Perhaps the chemistry between him and Modi echoed a friendship from another time? Could it be that Trump felt at home in India because something deep inside his unconscious memory recalled his life there long ago?

It is interesting to see how India has now become a country with significant international influence. I am reminded of how in 1897, Swami Vivekananda foresaw how India would rise to great heights again. He prophesized that "India, when independent, will embrace the materialism of the West and attain material prosperity to such an extent that it will surpass its past records in that field".

He also foresaw that "Countries such as America would become increasingly spiritual because they will have realized from the height of material prosperity the simple truth that gross materialism cannot give eternal peace." And later, to a group of American journalists, he said, "This is your century, but 21st century is India's century. Those barbarians and marauders who conquered us and plundered our Country would come back to our country to pay homage to our ancient sages and saints."

The hidden forces in Trump's Life

The Bhrigu explains the forces at work in Trump's life. Success does not come easy, but he will go to any length to fulfil his desires. Sometimes he can become furious, and he carries a lot of negative thinking. These qualities will bring him many health problems, which the Bhrigu says can be cured if he can focus his willpower through daily meditation and yoga. It would also help him to 'master his out of control senses and organs.'

Behind all of this lying, cheating, promiscuity, and ruthlessness, he lingers memories and enduring powers when he was a yogi. He must detach himself from his present materialistic life and once again seek spiritual power. There are still opportunities in his life; it says that will enable him to follow a higher path. 'Towards the end of his life, he can miraculously change his course towards spiritual understanding and inner happiness.'

Sadly, he may not hear or heed the advice of the Bhrigu, and he will face many humiliations. I will send him a copy of this book and hope that maybe he will discover solace in holy men like Sharavana Baba.

The Bhrigu continues: 'He should learn to be discreet and to control his senses. Due to his haughty nature, he feels superior to others. He feels insulted if he has to bend in front of others. He is very arrogant and ignorant. But destiny wants to teach him a great lesson, so destiny creates many situations in this lifetime so that he needs to bend in front of others.'

Instructions include ways that he can make spiritual changes that may spare him humiliation. Included are a series of remedies that need to be done by temple priests that will improve his health and peace of mind. He is also given some mantras to chant and amulets and gemstones that he must wear for his health and success.

Trump is next given a year by year list of events

that will happen in his life up to the time of his death. These details must remain unpublished here.

It also gives him some spiritual remedies that will extend the length of his life beyond his predicted death date. It talks about his marriages and children, as well as some incidents that will happen. There is information about his next reincarnation and future life. Included are essential remedies to be done, but 'since he will not hear my words, he will not perform them, and we cannot say with clarity what will happen.'

Trump's Future

When you consult the Bhrigu Samhita, you can also ask up to six questions. I asked about his reelection in 2020 and whether there is a real danger of assassination. However, the fact that he did not do the remedies as prescribed means that he would not be removed from office by impeachment but would not fulfil the second term. It was fascinating to see the emphasis in the Naadi about cheating and being cheated.

Interestingly there does seem to be a respite for him from an unexpected source. The Naadi says that he may not complete his presidency. These are the exact words: 'But by luck, he will succeed as he has the lady's luck. An older and spiritual or political lady will come forward to help him. She is a very powerful lady.' When we pressed the oracle for more details, the reply was: 'If not performing the suggested remedies, the opposite may happen, and then all his luck will turn against him, and even lady luck will not be there to help him, but the contrary will happen. :

He will continue his ill work and be remembered for lying and cheating.'He has committed several criminal acts and cheated. He is a notorious liar. However, if he changes his mindset and acts, he may by God's grace be able to turn himself towards a deep inner spiritual path, which will make everyone very surprised.'

In conclusion, Bhrigu reminds us that Trump must do the remedies. These will lift him to a higher spiritual level, improve his health, and extend his life. With this in mind, I have published the above and hope that somehow Trump may read this and undertake the essential remedies. These can be done without him being present but must be with his consent.

(The remedies to be performed by a Brahmin priest (or maybe even by Sharavana Baba) are The Nava Chandi Pooja, the Mangal, Ketu, and the Guru mantra Japa. Trump must do pooja to Lord Shiva every day and once a year during Maha Shivaratri plus the Rudra Abishekam and the Kalasarpa Pooja.)

Predictions for the Golden Age

Could there ever be a time when the whole world will be happy? We have seen so many great men and women walk the earth and spread enlightenment, but the world we see today appears as bad as ever. In the past, we had serfdom, slavery, plagues, famine, and wars, yet these same things persist in new and different forms. We are slaves to jobs, computers, materialism and our diets make us fat and lazy. Wars persist, and the danger of extinction from pandemics, wars, and environmental change is more significant than ever.

Today we have all this and more with lots of new unhappiness resulting from isolation, fear and self-doubt that arises from social media and the flawed values of the mainstream media. Amusements enslave our minds, our memory damaged by easy access to information, and incessant stimulus swamps our soul's peace. Indeed a happy world depends on a well-ordered society based on moral and spiritual values, not this endless rampage of trivia.

In the online world, we can block people and ideas we don't like and surround ourselves with those that agree with us, making us lopsided and unable to cope with the harsh realities of the real world. We do the same with our history by removing records of what we don't like and whitewashing the warnings of the past to fit with today's ideas. The world is getting more challenging as we become weaker and unable to deal with it.

It's hard to imagine a Golden Age where the world is perfect and happiness abounds. Yet, the ancient teachings of India assure us that the age of truth – the Sathya Yuga – will eventually happen. The timing is open to debate, but we can look for signs that herald its arrival.

The Vedas teaches that there are four ages—Satya, Treta, Dvapara, and Kali—that, like the seasons, repeat over and over again. Together they form a time unit known as the chaturanga that lasts for 8.64 million years. When the universe finally collapses on itself, another is created in its place.

The legends tell us that the whole human race was enlightened during the previous Age of Satya Yuga.

Everyone had mastery over the mind and projected compassion and love toward others. Most people's lives were spent in quiet meditation on the divinity within the heart during this age. People were fearless, content, and noble souls who had no attachment to materialism. All had superhuman powers and could obtain anything they wanted through the power of the will. Negative human traits were non-existent—these were times of heaven on Earth.

Sharavana Baba said to a small group of us gathered to listen to one of his discourses in London that "Meditation is done to reveal the knowledge of reality." Of course, there are many benefits to meditation, such as reducing stress, control of anxiety, increased memory and attention span, improved health and wellbeing, greater happiness and so on, but these can be a distraction. The goal is to awaken to reality.

In his talk, Sharavana Baba emphasizes that once we reach the goal of meditation, we become one with God, so there is no longer any need to do anything. No further effort is required. Techniques become obsolete, and so does the vanity of an inflated ego. Yet, in the same series of talks, he explained that we live in dangerous times when many evil people, such as terrorists, infest the earth. Because of this, it becomes imperative that we all take our spirituality to a new level by engaging in spiritual practice. This spiritual practice will raise the collective consciousness of humankind and thereby safeguard the future of the planet.

There is a long way to go before we reach the states of consciousness attained in Satya Yuga. Many prophets and seers say that we are now moving towards a New Age. Just as the darkness is darkest before dawn, the world will be troubled at this changing point, they say, but holy men and women will be born who will guide humanity to the goal.

I feel that we are on the threshold of momentous spiritual times and that many great beings are incarnating now who will lead us to unprecedented beautiful times. The triple incarnations of Sathya Sai Baba are the most obvious. Still, others – including Sharavana Baba, of course – will become the spiritual luminaries that will take us to unimaginable spiritual height.

Escaping the Robot Mind

Most people live a life of dull, mundane repetition. They are not awake and live like somnambulist robots. Some are so timid that the very thought of escaping from this grim routine is frightening. It is much better to hide by 'switching off'. Others prefer to get drunk or have a wild time and delude themselves into thinking that this is happiness. Life is not an all-you-can-eat buffet, and indulgence is just another way of denying happiness. All these things are attempts to avoid reality and return to primal unconsciousness.

Only the human form has the intelligence and discriminative faculty that gives it the capability of realizing the Divine Self. If we are alone in the universe, then we truly are at the Crown of Creation, and our opportunity is uniquely precious. Human birth is a rare piece of good luck and is our chance to attain knowledge and spiritual bliss, yet, of the millions of people that have passed this way, how few take this opportunity. If we would stop hiding and be what we truly are, which is embodiments of Divine Consciousness, then we would be incredibly happy.

Every excuse is made not to live fully: we tell ourselves that we work at a horrible job to support our children, think we can find true happiness in another person or that everything will be fine if we have more things. The list of ways to hide is very long. Most modern activities aim to escape these false securities, yet very few people want to switch off the monotonous robot and truly wake up. We look outside of ourselves for happiness and forget that real happiness lies within us.

Modern science is not very cheery either. It seeks to prove that we are all simply the byproducts of a purposeless universe and that our awareness is just a flash. Life is meaningless, and there is undoubtedly nothing after death. The grave is the end of things – get used to the idea. Eventually, even this vast clockwork universe will wind down and return to a void of darkness. Like you, it will be on more. Consciousness was just a blip.

But this is not what our heart tells us. We are not in denial when we feel the growing urge to dive deeper. Perhaps you have heard the heart's quiet voice trying to talk through the clatter of daily life. "There's more to it all than this," it whispers. "So much more." Something - you don't know quite what - calls you from within.

You know there is a journey to be taken. A journey to discover who you are and why you are here. You know that, as with any journey, there will be places where the path is steep and hard, as well as times when the landscape opens up to you in glorious splendour. Setting out takes some courage, and you will need a map and maybe a guru too.

Kalagnanam Prophecies

Some of my predictions I discovered had been similar to those found in an obscure (to Westerners) manuscript called the Kalagnanam (sometimes spelt Kaala Gnanam.) The Kalagnanam is a Sanskrit and also a Telugu word, which means 'Knowledge of Times' or 'Prophecy.' It is a work by multiple authors but, most importantly, has prophecies by Shree Veera Brahmendra Maha Swami, who some call the Indian Nostradamus.

He was born before the fall of the Chola dynasty, so his birthdate was sometime around the 9th Century AD. He had made many correct predictions in his lifetime and foresaw how the British East India Company would rule India. (His actual words were that the 'Swetha Mukham people would rule the land.')

When I first researched Shree Veera Brahmendra Maha Swami and the Kalagnanam texts, the prophecy that leapt out at me talked about a gas cloud that arises in China. I'd spoken about this in my YouTube channel several times and in my book 'Messages from the Universe.' My Naadi said that I would be the one who would alert people to its trajectory.

I had always interpreted this literally, but in retrospect, could this have been Coronavirus? Was it seen by both the Naadi and Shree Veera Brahmendra Maha Swami? I warned about a gas cloud and a pandemic that would sweep the world on my YouTube channel. In the same video, I had talked about a prelude to this being flocks of birds falling from the sky. This event happened just before the virus outbreak in December 2020 at Anglesey in Wales and then later in March in Missouri, USA and a flock of gulls dying en masse in Horowhenua, New Zealand.

I had often 'seen' this gas cloud in my meditations. It felt that the date would be around 2023 but could it be a symbolic representation of the virus? Indeed, people were saying this in the comments on my YouTube channel. Some of Shree Veera Brahmendra Maha Swami's Southern India followers claimed that in stanza 114, he had foreseen the Coronavirus. "Poisonous gas will emerge in the East. Lakhs of people will die. Coranki disease hits one crore people. Just like fumbling chicken, they will fall and die," he wrote.

Followers of the saint believe that coranki disease is a reference to Coronavirus. The connection to the East indicates that this pandemic's origin is China.

In the Kalagnanam, it says in verse 313 that 'by the power of mantras, miracles happen on earth.' It talks of many terrible calamities and the coming of a great Avatar (godman) who will establish peace on earth after the rise and fall of a false prophet. The Avatar's name is given as Veera Bhoga Vasanta Rayalu. In verse 292, it says, 'After rains fall thrice a month, men will live with ethics. On earth, dharma will be established. The order of God will be followed.'

All this is encouraging and in line with my feelings that we are on the edge of a golden age that we can quicken through with our spiritual work. The golden age dawns bit by bit as individuals are illuminated over a long period. If your heart is open and you do the work on yourself, then this is an auspicious time when you can awaken.

Good spiritual people like Sharavana and others are the heralds of the new times and are also the catalyst that can help trigger your illumination. The golden age can happen right now – inside you!

Returning to the Kalagnanam prophecies. It predicts some bleak events, some of which correspond to things I have already said. We will see the start of these times by the birth of a new star in the northern sky by 2024. I was writing this in 2020, so we do not have long to wait. A 'new star' must be something quite dramatic such as Supernova or a cosmic event visible to the naked eye. The star is said to have three tails.

Soon after the birth of the new star is the birth of the new Avatar in around 2025–26. Could this be the third incarnation of Sai Baba? I feel that Sai Baba may already be with us in my visions and has not revealed himself yet. I also think that the new Avatar will be so extraordinary that we cannot possibly understand him. He will be beyond human, and his words will be unintelligible to us. We will only be able to understand him through our intuition and telepathy. For most people, it will be impossible to be physically close to him as his energy will be so powerful and incomprehensible that it simply scrambles our thinking. According to the Kalagnanam, the Avatar is revealed to the world in 2037–38.

Many of the predictions are intertwined with some surreal prophecies. For example, verse 4 says, 'in Kamalapuram near Kadapa, the frog will shout like a hen.' And then later in verse 48, it says, 'In Kandukur woman becomes man, a stone hen will shout later.'

These are strange images that seem to make no sense. I am reminded that these verses come from multiple writers and – unlike Nostradamus – may be a mixture of differing talents.

Akashic Record

Indian philosophy teaches that all that has ever happened is recalled in the Akashic Record. The Sanskrit word akasha means 'open sky', representing an all-pervading field in the ether in which a record of past events is imprinted. This concept of a compendium of all universal events, thoughts, words, emotions, and intent ever to have occurred to all living beings was taken up by theosophy and anthroposophy and profoundly influenced Western mystical philosophy. Ancient and modern seers gain access to this 'universal mind' and knowledge of the past, present and future.

Every one of us has extraordinary potential. There are more connections between the dendrites and axons in our brain than all the particles in the universe. We can not only remember everything that has ever happened to us in every moment of our lives, but we also have substantial spare capacity. Under hypnosis, some people can recall past events in the minutest detail. Similarly, if electrodes stimulate parts of the brain, long-forgotten memories are recalled that are extraordinarily vivid. Subjects tested in this way describe the experience as reliving the past as if it were the present. The human mind works like a hologram with memory imprinted all over the brain. Every moment of our lives is there, but most of us have only limited access to this overwhelming amount of information.

Just as the brain may work as a hologram that retains vast amounts of information, so too the Akashic Record is holographic and has the imprint of everything that has ever happened. The ancients tell us that it also has a record of everything that will happen in the future.

If we had full access to this information, we would be overwhelmed and could not function. However, we can attune ourselves to this hidden knowledge through our intuition. Once we accept that it is possible to know things without study, we discover that we can also gain access to past, present and future, other realities, other places, and the world after death.

Ancient and modern-day seers all gain access to this vast reservoir, but we see only a part of it. We see "through a glass darkly," as the Bible says. The information we access has to be experienced rather than known rationally, and experience thereby colours our understanding and influences our prophecies of the future.

CHAPTER 17

To India

It is often the case that when you set out on a spiritual journey, there is a clearing of karma beforehand. Unforeseen and sometimes unpleasant events will happen, which are a way to clear the path ahead. Trouble knocked on our door in 1998 when Jane and I went to see Sathya Sai Baba in Puttaparthi, and on other occasions, I have embarked on a pilgrimage to the East. The last time I'd gone to India, I spent the weeks before leaving in a hospital on a blood transfusion drip recovering from anaemia.

Hindus pray to the god Ganesha before any critical undertaking or journey because he is believed to be the remover of all obstacles. Hence he is also hailed as Vighnaharta, wherein Vighna means barriers or hurdles. I did my chants, but perhaps I needed some stronger puja a few weeks before I left; we had some unexpected bad news: Jane's father was terminally ill and in hospital.

Jane's father was not the best of men. As a young man, he had been a cruel and selfish drunk and had deserted Jane's mother leaving her alone to bring up three children on her own with no money or support. For most of her life, Jane believed her Dad was dead. When Jane and I first met in 1987, we visited the Public Record Office at Kew in London, and we went through the National Archives to see if we could trace him or find his death certificate.

We found nothing until the advent of the internet, and I tracked him down in about 2016. Jane and I soon visited him – we drove upcountry and just turned up on his doorstep on a dark and rainy evening. It was an emotionally challenging experience after years of not knowing, but wounds were healed, and Jane forgave him for the many wrongs of the past. Sharavana often talks of the importance of respect towards our parents. "Even Gods bow to their parents," he says. "They should be given that much importance. Then only we become perfect. Today we are children; tomorrow, we will be parents. As you treat your parents, your children will treat you."

Jane would call her father from time to time, and we would visit him near Christmas. Calling him was often difficult, for it became apparent that some of the people in his household didn't want him in contact with us. He used to call Jane in secret from his mobile phone when he was at the bottom of the garden and out of sight. Something fishy was going on, but he lived far from us, so it was hard to keep tabs on precisely the problem. He was becoming much less lucid and vulnerable as time progressed and never volunteered what troubled him.

We left for the hospital immediately after we got the call from the nurse. He was already quite far gone when we arrived, but it was clear that nobody had visited him at all. His eyes burst into delight when she arrived. Jane gave him what comfort she could, although by now, it was clear that he was well on the path to passing to the next life. We were not able to be with him at the moment he died.

It was then that the troubles began. A double blow hit Jane when we discovered that a neighbour who had been helping with his care had the will made out to her alone. It had been a challenging emotional experience dealing with the death, but now we had legal matters on top. We were advised that there was nothing we could do without being drawn into what could be years of expensive legal disputes. Although her father had told us five years ago that he would change the will, it became clear that this had not happened. We realised that he's been under duress, hence the secret telephone calls, but there was no way we could prove it.

With all this unresolved stress and grief floating in the air, I made my preparations to go to India. Jane wanted me to continue with the plans. She would have loved to have gone too but nowadays found the long flights and the journey's pressures too much. I was going there to write a book but also as a representative of both of us. We knew that any blessing that Sharavana gave to me also extended to Jane too. He treated us as two souls as one.

Jane was magnanimous about all that had happened. "You go and enjoy the trip to see Sharavana," said Jane. "But I do insist on one task that you must do. You must buy me a glittery yellow sari!"

"It's a deal," I quipped. "A yellow sari shall be yours!"

Alison and Ash

The journey to India was a tough call. I'd booked a hotel at London Heathrow and woke up feeling thoroughly relaxed, fresh and ready to fly. I was travelling with Ash and his wife Alison, whom Jane and I had met through some of the Sharavana events in London. They had been to the ashram many times and owned an apartment on the site. Alsion enabled me to sort out accommodation at the ashram and helped me to plan everything for the journey. Apart from the usual nightmares you have to go through to get a visa to India, everything went smoothly. I met ash and Alison at the airport departure area, and all was well.

The couple had been followers of Sharavana for many years. They would make great travel companions and were refreshingly intelligent people and knowledgeable about Indian philosophy and customs. Sharavana had been the person who was the matchmaker in the relationship and helped them to find one another. The couple had even gotten married at the ashram some years before. So they knew the ropes. These would be my friends and guides through the pilgrimage to India.

All was going so well until the storm hit the airport. Early February 2020 saw Storm Ciara and Storm Dennis hit the UK in quick succession. It became one of the most intense extratropical cyclones ever recorded, reaching a minimum central pressure of 920 millibars. It was like the 'Beast from the East' created havoc with our trip to take Damian to see Sharavana in London. Why is it that whenever I go to see Sharavana, the weather turns surreal!

In an unexpected and sudden turn, an announcement told us that all flights were cancelled. Instantly all of the airport hotels and all nearby hotels were fully booked. We were stranded and would probably have to sleep on the airport floor. I could feel the freshness falling from me as I prepared myself for an arduous journey to India.

Alison believed that if you chant Saravanabhava three times in a row with deeply felt sincerity, any obstacle will fall away. She had already demonstrated this to me when we waited in a long queue. Three chants later, an airport official closed one row and summoned us to the front of a new row, and we were now first in line.

"We have to all chant 'Om Saravanabhava' three times together, and all will be well", she assured us. There was nothing to lose, and it beat sleeping on the airport floor.

Nothing happened. Then Alison had an epiphany. "I've got it!" she said excitedly. "It's come to me; we know a devotee near to the airport. I'm sure I must have his address here somewhere."

An hour later, we were on our way to Krishna's house. He was more than happy to put us up and even took us all out to a top restaurant for quality vegetarian mean. Our fortunes seemed to have suddenly reversed with a chant that seemed to open Alison to inspiration and attracted a lovely man who was keen to help us.

And it certainly beat the prospect of an airport

floor. Krishna was a multi-millionaire and lived in a mansion in a gated community with pop stars for neighbours. We spent the night in luxury with an evening of animated conversations about the miracles of Sharanana Baba. Krishna had a magnificent pooja room dedicated to Sharavana, and I learnt Sharavana would often come and stay here when he visited London.

It's remarkable how powerful that mantra can be.

The shattering journey.

Dubai Airport, our first stop on the way to India, is the world's busiest airport by international passenger traffic and, just like Heathrow, is a fine example of materialism on steroids. It is adorned with golden palm trees and has all the top brands selling at high prices. We found a seat and ate a few overpriced sandwiches as white-robed Arabs in sunglasses floated past us like Daleks on the shiny floors. There were hours to go before our connecting flight.

Airports are corporate propaganda. They are a deliberate statement of a country's success and key to a country's national and international trade relations. However, so often, when you leave an airport, you see the stark contrast between the affluence of an environment made for wealthy fliers and the reality of the country itself. We didn't leave the airport, but it set me thinking about the implications of this shiny world and the experience of India ahead.

Most people confuse happiness with gratification. If we get what we want, we are happy. If we don't, then we are sad. When gratification comes, there is a momentary easing of dissatisfaction, and for a short time, it feels as if unhappiness is conquered. The snag is that the background feeling of unease and a lack of contentment returns, and soon we are back on the treadmill searching to satisfy our material desires.

Pleasure-based happiness is usually a selfish pursuit. A narrow pursuit of sensual happiness can bring many negative mental states associated with selfishness, such as cruelty, violence, pride, greed and so on. A selfish search for this limited type of happiness can bring a great deal of unhappiness for everyone else. It can also never be permanently satisfied, so it leaves the seeker forever unfulfilled.

Perhaps greater happiness would come to us of itself if we could somehow get rid of this background feeling of unease. For others, unhappiness may be an essential trait that is strangely necessary. For example, Edvard Munch, who painted the harrowing image of The Scream, was asked why he did not do something about his emotional problems. He replied: "They are part of me and my art. They are indistinguishable from me, and it would destroy my art. I want to keep those sufferings." For many people, of course, depression and negative thinking can quickly become a trap that they find hard to escape. The only way to break free of negativity is to invite in positivity. You can't escape the prison of negativity by constantly thinking about it.

I took a bite of my Pret A Manger vegetarian wrap and thought about how it would be interesting to explore the concept of happiness as I make my pilgrimage to India. The dismal wrap tasted like horsehair mashed up with Crème Fraiche with all the flavour removed. It spoke of dejection, melancholy and a dash of sorrow. This was junk food at its finest.

There are problems with seeking happiness in gratification, of course. You can't always get what you want, and if you do get what you think you want, it just increases your attachment to it and binds you even more to suffering and dissatisfaction. And of course, even if you get all the things you want, there will still be more things to crave, such as power, wealth, name and fame.

Looking at the airport, I could see that the corporate world is geared up to exploit unhappiness and dissatisfaction. Our weakness is to think that happiness comes by adding something to our lives. We feel that something is missing, so we naturally try and fill the gap.

Even when we find some fleeting happiness, many fear expressing their joy. We sat, and 'people watched'. A group of Chinese people passed us, and I am reminded of their proverb, "extreme happiness begets tragedy". Behind them is a striding group that looks like they may be Russian. In Russia, they say that anyone happy or prosperous has used immoral means to get results – so avoid them! Following them is a group of Iranians. Many Iranians believe in the 'evil eye' and that one should be very careful about showing happiness in public or someone's envy may curse you. Before talking about something good, many Iranians will say, "may the devil's ear be deaf" to thwart misfortune.

It is a shame that many of us from all nations do not express our happiness as indeed a joy shared is a joy doubled. But I can empathise with some of these superstitions, as I, too, have met many people who are jealous of another's happiness and will do everything in their power to destroy it. Being happy can cause bad luck as it triggers resentment in others.

Instead of comparing themselves with others, these mean-minded people should discover what true happiness is and then seek to remove the cause of their own unhappiness. No one is going to hand you happiness; you have to work for it. For example, it is possible to remove insecurity, the need for approval, envy, greed, discontent, and so on by replacing them with contentment, gratitude, acceptance, service to others and non-greed.

Seeking happiness is a false path. The act of seeking is the opposite of happiness. Happiness is always here, never somewhere else. It is always within ourselves. For this reason, we must never carry a fear of suffering as it will burden our progress. Never fear what will happen on the path ahead. Have no fear of suffering. With a fearless heart, explore the highest roads of life, and happiness will be your eternal travelling companion.

I would undoubtedly probe some of these ideas during my journey to holy India.

The hours slipped by, and soon we were through security. With a few 'Om Sharavana Baba's from Alison, we put at the front of the queue and soon seated in the plane and on our way to India.

Arriving Kerala

I was pretty impressed with Kerala. It's certainly not as poor and rubbish-strewn as I'd seen in other areas of India. Bombay was a mess, so was Bangalore, Delhi, Calcutta and Chennai, but Kerala gave quite a good first impression. The airport was modern, clean and well organised. There is the usual 'Check Point

Charlie' ordeal at customs, but this is India, and it's to be expected. Getting a visa for India was a nightmare by the way – if you decide to follow my trail, make sure you plan months in advance as the visa websites are a labyrinth. And another tip: buy an Indian phone card when you arrive at the airport so that local and international calls are cheaper.

As we drove towards the ashram, I could see that Kerala was much more affluent than I'd seen elsewhere. For a start, it had proper roads. It was likely that I'd survive this journey. This outing was not going to be like the terrifying drives I'd taken in Northern India on perilously dangerous roads in the Himalayas, skating on the broken tarmac and slippery dirt roads.

"I suggest you get some sleep on the way," said Alison. "It's going to be a four to five-hour drive."

Sleep was, of course, impossible. I was in the front seat and was keen to see all the new scenes of India unfolding. Kerala is beautiful and safe. It is famous for its beaches, temples, backwaters and food. Compared to the dry landscapes I'd seen in Southern India, this place was lush. Malayalam is the local language (which is not dissimilar to Tamil), and the word 'keralam' – from which the name Kerala derives - translates as 'land of the coconut tree'. The emerald backdrop of palms and coconuts interspaced by stretches of rivers, waterways and small lakes accompanied us the whole journey.

Most surprising were the number of Christian Churches on the route. Christianity is the third-most practised religion in Kerala. It has been practised here since the arrival of Saint Thomas at the ancient seaport Muziris on the Kerala coast in AD 52. Vasco da Gama followed in 1498 and opened the floodgates to European colonialism and Arab traders. The original Christian community were mainly merchants, and today the tradition continues in the incongruous shops that lined some of the roads. I could see Christian funeral shops with headstones and garish grave goods of all types and a vast array of coffins with stylish linings in pink, white or a dashing funereal mauve.

Many Christian religious icon shops also sold full-size statues of Jesus and the saints with windows stuffed full of garish icons. I hadn't seen anything like this since visiting the Vatican. One had a sign in English saying 'Open All Hours. All very useful if you suddenly discover that you've run out of blue flock covered madonnas or need to dash out and get some holy water from the local shop in the middle of the night.

In India, you must expect the unexpected.

In some countries, they drive on the left-hand side of the road, and in a few countries, they go on the right-hand side. In India, they drive in the middle of the road. The drive was not as bad as I had experienced in other areas of India, and at least the road was tarmacked. In some places, there are potholes you could lose your car in. Everywhere the rule is each vehicle for themselves with lorries and busses dominating and taking up to three lanes at a time. The main problem is the sheer amount of traffic on the roads. Few drivers follow any rules other than biggest wins! You see cows, elephants, autorickshaws and whole families on tiny motorcycles while huge old Leyland lorries force their way through the lot.

Gradually the towns made way to villages; the

roads became smaller and dustier. Finally, the landscape opened into a rolling terrain of waving palms and a cascade of lush green vegetation. We drove through a run-down village of concrete shops with flashy signs and eventually approached the arch that marked the ashram entrance.

"Once we have booked in and sorted out the rooms," said Alison, "we can, if we are quick, catch the afternoon Dharshan. You should be able to talk to swami."

Where is Shakti?

The air was sultry and weighty with warmth as we entered the ashram's brightly coloured temple area. The harsh squawks of peacocks cut through the din of the noisy temple soundscape. The smoke of sandalwood incense billowed in curves through the sun rays that streamed through the open-sided building. On every wall and pillar were images and carvings of brightly painted gods and goddesses. I could hear distant drumming and music, and to my right, I caught sight of the nearby jungle's emerald colours. It felt now that I was in India. I had finally arrived.

At the far side of the temple, I could see the figure Sharavana. He was dressed in brightly coloured robes and sat on a golden chair as people knelt before him to get his help. Some people left as others remained to make a long line in front of Sharavana to receive his blessing and get a short personal message from their guru. It is customary to give him a small token gift such as a piece of fruit, some joss sticks, betel leaves, and so on. I took some candy. He then redistributes these by giving a present back to whoever sits in front of him.

Ash and I joined the long queue and - well out of earshot of Swami - got drawn into an in-depth discussion. Ash is intelligent and knowledgeable, so it was enjoyable to have the chance to talk about spiritual things as we waited our turn to see Sharavana. Up until this point, most of our discussions had been about the practical problems of our travel.

We started chatting and somehow ended up talking about whether the highest reality –Brahman - is identical with Ātman - the inner self, spirit, or soul. It was quite an entwined discussion about duality and non-duality and not the sort of conversation that often envelopes you in normal conversation back home. Not many people think about these things, let alone want to chat about them. Here, the energy was high and spiritual discussion was the default mode of communication.

I argue that as I prove the continuation of the human personality after death with my mediumship, then clearly, something does persist and must have an independent existence. As put forward by people such as Ramana Maharshi and philosophers from the Advaita Vedanta traditions, the contrary argument is that when we ask 'who and I?' all we will find is the absolute reality and nothing more. The Buddha also argued that 'the self is empty of inherent existence.' I concluded by suggesting that maybe both realities coexist in a symbiotic paradox that is impossible for anybody to comprehend.

In our chat, we also talked about the two opposed but complementary forces of Shiva and Shakti. (Shiva symbolises consciousness, the masculine principle and Shakti represents the feminine principle, the activating power, and energy.) Eventually, we fell into silence and gathered our thoughts as the long queue gradually shortened.

At last, I found myself knelt before Sharavana Baba, and as usually happens, we both fell into a slightly silly and humorous mood. When he visited our house or saw him at public events, we laughed together like two adolescent schoolboys.

'Hello Shiva,' he says. 'Where's Shakti?'

For a moment, he caught me completely off balance as he had repeated the topic of the conversation I'd just been having with Ash. I should be used to this by now, but it always catches me by surprise. On one occasion, when Jane, our daughter Danielle and me met him in London, he repeated the conversation we'd had in the car nearly word for word.

'Oh, oh, I see. You mean, where is my wife Jane?' I said. As the penny dropped, we both fell into giggles. 'I'm afraid she cannot come, Swami. The journey would have been too much for her. She sends her love.'

He looks down and to the side and puckers his lower lip to look like a disappointed child. I hand him the sweets/candy.

'Ah!' he says as his face light up with a beamish grin. He draws me close and as if telling me a secret says, 'These sweets are sweet on the inside and beautiful on the outside.'

He looks me in the eye and says, 'Just like Atman and Brahman.'

'Be like sweets. Be happy, be happy, be happy!'

Hidden Clairvoyance

Even a few moments with Sahravana leave you in a spiritual swirl. It's hard to describe unless you've been there, but darshan with these saints is like coming down after taking a strange drug. It was just the same after Jane, and I had a hug from hugging saint Mata Amritanandamayi Devi, better known as Amma. I walked away afterwards, staggering like a drunk, whereas Jane, who had a leg injury, walked away like an athlete. Energy is exchanged that is transcendent of and words that are said.

With Sharavana Baba, the energy is always cheerful, and often we have hilarious exchanges. Being with him is as natural as being with one of your best friends. I remember him saying to Jane, 'I've waited for many incarnations for you,' and Jane replied, "Yes, and you owe me money from the previous incarnation!"

It's not the usual thing you'd say to a revered holy man, but Sharavana laughed like anything. He has such a wonderful sense of humour, and Jane knows that he doesn't mind if you have a joke with him.

Sharavana's words also clearly contained a great deal of clairvoyance as there was no possible way he could have overheard our conversations. In itself, clairvoyance is no big deal. Jane and I do it all the time with our work. However, what I find so astonishing is not only the flawless accuracy of Sharanavana Baba's powers but the scale of them.

There are numerous accounts of him whispering startling and accurate facts about the people kneeling before him. He will describe their lives and know the events that have happened in their lives. He knows their intimate thoughts, hopes, dreams, and hidden feelings. What he reveals is always helpful and uplifting. You feel showered with the steadfast, supportive, positive, and loving energy that people of the highest spiritual calibre only radiate. Many people become overwhelmed by his words, love, and spiritual presence and will often burst into tears.

His connection with devotees and newcomers alike is always deeply personal and unique and does this for hundreds of people, sometimes thousands, every day. He never tires.

If I do four private readings in a day or one spiritualist church demonstration of mediumship, I am exhausted for days afterwards. Sharavana not only does an incredible amount, but he also zaps every visitor full of energy. His energetic resources appear to be inexhaustible. His helpers who travel with him have told me that they are full of high energy levels when they are with him and can complete incredible amounts of work. As soon as they are away from him again, they crash. This unprecedented energy is, in my opinion, one of the hallmarks that single Sharavana out as an extraordinary being.

How many days was it since I'd slept properly? Probably about five, but I was feeling quite energised now. The sensible me was saying that it is essential that I now return to my room, shower, eat, and sleep, but sometimes enthusiasm gets the better of me.

Ash showed me around the ashram grounds and before meeting up with his wife, Alison.

'Ash and I are going back to our room now,' said Alison as we walked back towards the living quarters. 'I heard that Swami is taking people to the Naga snake temple in the jungle. It has been abandoned for a while, so they will be cleaning it up first. I strongly suggest you get some sleep, but if you did want to go, the bus is over there and about to leave.'

An abandoned Naga Temple? Snakes? Jungle!! It was just too 'Indiana Jones' for me to miss. Moments ago, I was tired beyond belief, but now I was raring to go. I dashed for the jam-packed ashram bus and made it just before the doors closed.

'Make sure you take plenty of mosquito repellent,' I heard Alison call out as the bus set off and roared towards the jungle.

The Sun dropped below the horizon; the sky darkened as the mosquitoes rubbed their tiny eyes to wakefulness and sharpened their bloodsucking probosci. With my face squeezed against the glass, I realised that I was tired beyond belief, and the jungle with all its charms awaited me.

The bus journey was, of course, chaotic and dangerous. Driving in India always is, but this driver must have special dangerous driving awards. Someone told me later that he also drove Sharavana's car – at breakneck speed. Resistance is futile. You must just go with the flow of India's mad roads, or you'll have a nervous breakdown. So with my tired face pressed against the glass of the window, I watched the strange world of India world flash past and thought of my comfy bed back home.

I'm exaggerating, of course. The journey wasn't that bad, and I was soon roused to wakefulness when the bus went off-road and thundered down narrow dusty dirt tracks and plunged through forests trails. There was still enough light to see the canopies of palm trees silhouetted against the darkening sky and get glimpses of animals scurrying away from us. And even here in a place free from traffic, the driver kept his hand always on the horn and scattered flocks of birds as we hit the dirt tracks at max speed.

Come to think of it; I wasn't exaggerating.

Snake Temple in Jungle

Fortunately, many Indian people speak English very well - India now claims to be the world's second-largest English-speaking country – and although there appeared to be no westerners aboard the bus, I was soon making friends.

One person I discovered came from Bournemouth – a seaside town that's less than an hour's drive from my home in the UK. He told me that he'd read my book *'God is Everywhere*, and we soon chatted, and he explained the objective of the journey as we stepped out of the bus and into the clearing in the trees.

'This Naga temple has become overgrown and a little neglected,' says the devotee. Our first task will be to clean it and prepare the ground. This should take a couple of hours, and then Swami will arrive, and he will perform some of the Naga rituals suitable for this small temple.'

The temple was not quite what I'd pictured in my imagination. It was set in an area about 30ft by 20ft clearing in the jungle with a central walled-off area entered by an ornate gate. Inside this were three 2ft high platforms on which stood three stone sculptures of coiled cobras. In front of this were two large stone stands – called Nachiarkoil or Annam lamps – on which camphor lights and incense sticks would be placed.

My immediate reaction to leaving the bus was to

walk towards the area and take a look.

'Oh, no, no, no, sir! Please take sandals off. Even the jungle floor is sacred ground,' said a woman who was sweeping the jungle floor with a coconut jhadu broom.

Not a good start as I had immediately put my foot in it but nobody minded, and I began barefooted to help with whatever I could – which wasn't much as I didn't have a clue about what goes where.

The whole area is surrounded by a high canopy of tall trees filled with birds and scurrying tree animals that made more noise as the Sun gradually set. After a couple of hours of everyone clearing foliage, sweeping the ground, and preparing the lights and pooja materials, Sharavana Baba arrived by car.

By now, it was dark, and the jungle around felt mysterious and unknown. Strange birds were calling as we chanted mantras. Wafts of thick scented incense passed gently through the warm air and cut the light beams from the makeshift lighting. Crickets echoed all around as the drums began, and we chanted 'Om Hreem Namah Shivaya.' This traditional Sanskrit mantra is considered by yogis to be particularly powerful because it invokes the spirit of both Lord Shiva and Shakti, existing as a divine couple in eternal bliss. This mantra and many others will be chanted over the coming days and nights until the final ceremonies on the night of Maha Shivaratri.

Sharavana has a beatific smile. He was dressed in majestic attire of turquoise green and gold. He walked through the gate in front of the temple area and, together with his assistants, performed several poojas. Most of the poojas involved bells, fire, and flowers. There were many bursts of chanting, music, and mantras, as well as moments of quiet and meditation. The most important and visually exciting part of the ceremonies involved pouring vast amounts of yellow ochre turmeric over the three Snake idols (Naga).

I joined in the clapping and mantras, and as the vibrations lifted to a height, a thought struck me: I had forgotten my insect repellent.

I'm not sure if the word had got around the mosquito community that I was there, but once it was dark, they were there in their millions to sample my pale white skin. I stood as a beacon of incandescence like the only restaurant on a lonely road through the night. I could hear them buzzing around me and placing their orders.

We were quite tightly closed in on one another as we clapped and chanted, but hopefully, no one would notice as I clapped my hands then slapped my neck, face, legs, or arms to clear the bloodsucking army. It took some skill to simultaneously keep in rhythm, chant a mantra, and slap away a mosquito horde. Now I know how lederhosen-clad Germans feel when they slap their legs, sing, drink beer, and dance in perfect synchronicity to Oom-pah bands.

I was just getting into the rhythm when my hand struck something solid at about the height of my elbow. In the darkness, I had slapped a little old lady around the head. She yelped and laughed as I made my embarrassed apologies.

This was my first encounter with Sharavana's mother.

The Naga

The idea of worshipping snakes does not come easy to many Westerners brought up within a Christian background. Snakes are associated with temptation, poison, threat, hidden danger, lies, vengefulness, vindictiveness, and evil. Nonetheless, they have been worshipped for thousands – perhaps millions - of years and have many positive connotations. We see the snake as the brass image of a serpent coiled around a rod in the staff of Moses. Those who looked upon the serpent were healed. Snakes are the symbols of healing and medicine seen in the caduceus of Hermes and the Rod of Asclepius. In Mesopotamia, the serpent was also associated with healing deities.

In Genesis, the serpent is depicted as a trickster who promotes as good what God had forbidden. It is a symbol of cunning and deception and yet is also the bringer of knowledge. The implication in the story is that God created the snake so that we would seek knowledge. It is our free will to act, but we fall from innocence and enter the dualistic world of experience by so doing.

Snakes are also a symbol of transcendence that occurs in many cultures throughout the world. Therefore, it is a creature of the underworld and is the mediator between one way of life and another. The Greek god Hermes was called 'psycho-pomp,' meaning soul-guide. He and his incarnation in the Roman god Mercury would guide the souls of the dead to the underworld carrying the caduceus. The caduceus also has wings showing how it is associated with birds as a symbol of transcendence. The underworld snake consciousness attains transcendence to the superhuman state of divine awakening.

The snake is also associated with the phallus and sexual energy. In kundalini yoga, the energy at the base of the spine - the Muladhara chakra - is represented by a coiled snake. While sexual desire is generated at the level of svadhisthana chakra, sexual vitality is a function of the Muladhara chakra. The Kundalini is a form of divine feminine energy (or shakti) that can be awakened to join with its counterpart Shiva that resides at the crown of the head (Sahasrara chakra).

Sharavana tells us that "Serpent worship delivers the inner courage to lead a life in accordance with the rhythms of the cosmos."

As I watched the nocturnal ceremonies, I was fascinated by how ancient many of these poojas and rituals must be. Animalistic rituals involving snakes were probably part of the first prehistoric religions where snakes were seen as entities of strength and renewal. People could have been doing these same rituals many thousands of years ago.

My investigations into the Naadi oracles, the Bhrigu Samhita, and Vedic astrology have charged me to have various remedies performed involving snakes, so I felt comfortable with all that was going on. In one remedy prescribed by the Naadi, I had to do poojas to counter the harmful effects of Rahu.

Rahu is one of the nine major astronomical bodies (navagraha) in Indian astrological texts. Astrologically, Rahu is counted as a planet symbolised by the head of a mythological snake whose tail is Ketu, his planetary counterpart. In one of his discourses, Sharavana explained that we need to pay homage to Rahu at particularly auspicious times. Rahu is sometimes considered unfavourable, particularly if placed in the 7th house, but its influence is essential. The blood, he explained, moves around the body because of pressure. Without pressure in the blood, we would not live.

The timing of these rituals is kept secret and only known to awakened beings. They are usually performed at night and, like this ritual we were doing at the temple today, are announced without any prior notification. Sharavana also explained in other discourses that Rahu is part of the life force that we need to exist. Rahu and the snakes should also be likened to nature and the forest gods. Poojas to them will give us fearlessness.

I suggested elsewhere that the importance of snakes may have other mysterious origins. Could it be that snake people brought knowledge to humankind? Were these visitors from another planet or dimension? Some whacky ideas are floating around the Internet about lizard people, but there are many references to encounters with snake people in the mythology of Hinduism.

The word 'Naga' comes from the Sanskrit for a serpent or snake, especially the King cobra. In legends, the Naga is a semi-divine race of half-human half-serpent beings residing in the heavenly Patala and occasionally take human form. They are powerful beings who are both magnificent and proud, and their world is a place filled with gems, gold, and treasures.

The Naga are often associated with water, such as rivers, lakes, seas, and wells. Back at the ashram, they have a large pit that floods from underwater spring water at certain times. It is the area associated with the Naga and the spirits of the fearsome Aghori yogis who Sharavana Baba said once lived at that spot.

In Hindu mythology, the snake Vasuki, a Nagaraja, became the churning rope for the churning of the Ocean of Milk. Vasuki is famous for coiling around Shiva's neck, who blessed and wore him as an ornament. Because of a snake's nature of shedding its skin, it is seen as a symbol of rebirth and associated with several gods and goddesses. For example, Vishnu performs yoga Nidra (conscious sleep) on the gigantic cosmic snake called Shesha Nag. (Adishesha) In the Puranas, it is written that Shesha holds all the planets of the Universe on his hoods. He continually sings of the glories of the God Vishnu from all his mouths. (Again, I find these references to snakes in space intriguing and wonder if there may be some literal references here to Von Daniken's ancient aliens.)

As well as the snake Vasuki, other snakes appear in the holy texts and have temples dedicated to them. Kaliya was a ferocious poisonous snake with a hundred and ten hoods that lived in the Yamuna river and was subdued by the dancing Krishna. The goddess Mansa Devi governs snakes and is worshipped for the prevention and cure of snakebite as well as for fertility and prosperity.

The Nagas are revered in southern India, where it is believed that they bring fertility and prosperity to all who take part in these fascinating ceremonies. Meanwhile, the tiredness was beginning to hit home. The ceremonies lasted far longer than I had expected, and I was beginning to look like the walking dead.

When everything was complete, we all queued in front of Sharavana Baba, and he sprinkled a little of the Turmeric from the poojas into our open palms.

"Eat some of this every day for seven days and until Maha Shivratri," he said. "This is very important. It will bring health and improvement in your energy."

It was wonderful that I had witnessed all these mysterious nocturnal rituals but I was now so tired that I was hard to stand up. I had definitely over done things so it was nice to get back in the bus, sit down and be driven back safely to the ashram. I was able to get a seat right at the front so that I could watch India unfold as I dozed.

Crazy drive

It was late, and I'm sure the driver was keen to get back to his bed too. The vehicle squealed to a start. I'm sure smoke must have been streaming from the burning tyres as we lurched through the gears and into top speed. I grabbed my seat and clenched my teeth. This was going to be another white-knuckle ride into the unlit roads and wild oncoming traffic. Night driving was all the more terrifying as you just didn't know what was coming next. Suddenly there's the loud honk of a horn, the swerve of the vehicle, and headlights illuminate our darkness as another potential accident belts past our windows.

I flicked on my Insta360 camera, which films in all directions at once. When I reviewed the recording later, it was amusing to watch the near misses on the road in front, and the looks of absolute terror on the passengers' faces sat behind me. We all looked like startled animals about to become roadkill.

I eventually got back to the room and collapsed,

fully dressed face down onto the bed. As sleep stampeded towards me, I noticed that my face was pressed against hot polythene. They had been kind enough to give me a brand-new bed with its wrapping still in place. The bed was as hard as glass, the room was baking hot, I needed a shower, and my teeth were furry, but who cares?

CHAPTER 18

Indian Ashram

'Tiredness can be an obstacle to happiness', I thought as I prised myself from bed to begin my morning yoga. Now don't get me wrong, I was enjoying my stay in India, but I still looked like the walking dead, and it set me thinking about how vital our health and vitality are to spiritual awakening. I've been doing yoga since I was an adolescent and try to do it every day. I fail miserably but do manage to practice properly at least times a week if life is busy and more when I have the time. Ashram life gives us time, and fortunately, there was enough space in my room to lay out my mat where I could grunt and gyrate into my asanas.

In many of his talks, Sharavana has stressed that before we can embark on a spiritual path, we must first look after our health. "Health good?" is usually one of the first things he says when you meet him. Without good health, the path can become very difficult. This advice is, of course, why yoga and the breathing exercises called pranayama are so crucial as they prepare the body and astral body for the awakening process.

In the West, yoga is completely misunderstood, and most people wrongly believe that it is a form of exercise. Although the asanas of yoga will bring health, this is just a secondary benefit as the primary goal of yoga is to transcend the illusion of the physical. The clue is in the word 'yoga', which in Sanskrit literally means 'union. ' In the Yoga Sutras, Patanjali explains that yoga is the union between you and the divine, the cosmic being, consciousness, the universal principle, God or whatever you want to call it that in Sanskrit is called Purusha.

Fortunately, even the superficial practitioner of yoga may catch on to the idea that 'Happiness is an inside job.' Even if you don't understand how to meditate, simply closing your eyes will help a person internalise the attention. If you can then train the mind to concentrate so that the whirl of our internal dialogue can subside, this allows our true nature to emerge. Eventually, we discover that our true nature is happy, blissful and filled with indescribable peace. And yet, even this can be transcended. The final goal lies in an absolute state of cosmic consciousness beyond even the desire to know God or be Enlightened. It comes without effort as a divine gift.

Meanwhile, here back on Earth, we can work with yoga techniques to prepare ourselves for divine revelation. For many people, a mantra is a good starting point. The everyday mind is like a chattering monkey or a bored child that needs constant attention. We give it a mantra to distract its attention so that the real you can get on with the spiritual work. The comedian Russell Brand likens it to shutting up a boisterous child by handing it a PlayStation. There are many other methods to train the mind to become still, but a mantra is a good starting point if you are new to the path.

Our consciousness has evolved over millions of years and has changed. Archaic people would have thought, felt, and experienced the world in a very different way. This way of thinking is hard for us to imagine, as today we know only the awareness we have inherited. We know no other way of thinking or perceiving the world. Our assumption is that awareness is simply awareness, and it has always been this way. However, when we examine our awareness, we see that it can take many forms and has weight.

Awareness can be clear and rational, drenched with kindness and empath, filled with hate, darkness and fear. Sometimes in ourselves, we may feel fully awake and filled with insights and knowledge, but at other times, we fall into dull thoughts and the drab routines of the robotic mind. Some people we meet are bright and alive, some seem dark and withdrawn, and many appear almost asleep. Even in our everyday lives, we notice many differences in the way consciousness manifests.

Long ago, the way we thought and felt must have been very different to what we know now. Like the human body, consciousness had to evolve and go through many experimental prototypes, some of which became part of our modern selves and others obsolete. There is no fossil record of the evolution of consciousness, so we do not know if this awakening process happened gradually or in a sudden leap. We can only speculate about how or why consciousness evolved.

Our distant ancestors probably had a very different relationship with their thoughts than we do to ours. We have thoughts, and they are something that we feel we have control over and we believe are created by our volition. Consciousness in its infancy would not have had this same centre of awareness but would be rooted in reactive behaviour. Thoughts, ideas and feelings arose of their own accord out of nothing and came into the attention like ghosts, spirits or messages from the gods. In this twilight of consciousness, there would have been a minimal distinction between the inner and outer world. Both were much the same, with thoughts arising from within but appearing to be like messages coming from somewhere outside.

Sharavana gives the simple advice that we must live from the inside and not be constantly distracted by the things of the world. If we always seek in the world, we will be continuously disappointed as we are seeking happiness in the wrong place. We must remain focused within and make every experience part of our meditation. He says: "Mindfulness is essential. Life must be lived mindfully,"; "Be in a meditative state all the time! There must be power in your sight! Pursue spiritual practice relentlessly! Develop positive affirmation! Bask in the Divine Presence! Quieten the mind! Absorb the power of silence!"

The Restless Mind

Now don't get me wrong. My room was superb and pretty well; everything was brand new. But you know how it is. Once you fall into a cycle of restlessness and become overtired, even the comfiest environments feel like an ordeal. As I pulled the sweaty polythene off the new mattress, I noticed the label read 'Super orthopaedic extra-hard punishment mattress' – or something like that, I can't quite remember.

It was early morning, and my mind was still in the twilight zone. Jet lag and over-tiredness invariably result in a loss of mental focus that I find put the mind into an over-thinking state. My brain would not switch off as I laid down to sleep.

Overthinking is a common issue that upsets many people today. Our obsession with social media compounds it. The face we see when we go to sleep, and the one we look at when we wake up is invariably not our partner's but Facebook. Overthinking is habitual, and many hours are lost ruminating about the past and worrying about the future. Insignificant minor problems can get blown out of proportion by the skilled over-thinker so that they awake exhausted and unprepared for a new day. One of the leading causes of this modern epidemic is because we have lost control over our attention. Developing a regular meditation practice that includes concentration techniques is a proven way to help clear your mind of nervous chatter by turning your attention inward.

I had assumed that the incredibly loud chanting and squealing instruments that shook us awake at dawn were the calls to start the day. It sounded like snake charmers, maddened elephants, and amateur bagpipers were stampeding my dreaming mind. I found out later that the cleaners liked to play loud music over the PA system when they began their chores. I was most familiar with Sathya Sai Baba's ashram at Puttaparthi that I visited in 1997. The days there began at 3:00 am with a cold shower and frantic dash to get in the queues for darshan. Here, it was far more relaxed. There was no pressure to get up at dawn, and you could take everything at your own pace. But I didn't know that.

It was 4:00 am, and the granite of the bed didn't feel that enticing anymore, so I vouched for a few hours of yoga and meditation while I waited for Ash to message me on Whatsapp. He would show me around the ashram and familiarise me with the place and the ashram routines.

"Did you sleep well?" asked a chirpy looking Ash when he arrived. I wish now I'd take Alison's advice instead of spending most of the night with the serpent world.

"Sort of," I replied. "I managed a few hours, but I'm still quite jetlagged."

"Never mind, you'll adjust soon. What we'll do is head down to the temple complex, and I'll show you the routine that most people and I do when we are here. Various things happen all day and into the evening, and you can join in as you want. It's quiet now, so this is a good time to get to know the place. As Maha Shivaratri approached, the place will begin to get very busy."

Saravanabhava Madam

As we headed to the temple area of the ashram, we passed a group of small huts that Ash told me were put there so that wandering sadhus and holy men can find shelter. I glimpsed a few of these orange-clad mendicants washing and going about the daily business as we passed the dwellings but never saw them again during my stay. They are very reclusive people spending their time - I assume - in meditation and other spiritual pursuits.

Today, many of the 'holy men' in orange robes you see in India are simply ordinary beggars who know that they can increase their yield by donning the garb of a renunciant. I anticipate that Saharvana Baba only allows genuine holy men into the lodgings.

We wandered past a large hall used for public events and downhill past the kitchens and dining area to the temple area. The track takes us downward on a dusty track to a large two-story open-sided building decorated with a multitude of brightly painted gods and goddesses that entwine the glazed patterned pillars that support the opulent ceilings of the temple. It looked spectacular in the golden morning light.

Ash explained that devotees pay their respects to all of the shrines in a set order. This procedure should start your daily routine. You can choose what time you do this, but if you time it well, you will also see Sharavana Baba performing various poojas at the shrines.

As we enter the temple, we are greeted by the tiny figure of Sharavana's mother, who was beaming a big smile and seemed non the worse for the beating I'd given her at the snake temple.

The Sri Maha Ganapathi faces eastward with a lush green view of paddy fields and plantain plantations. I could see the feathers of a few bright blue peacocks catch the morning light as they moved through foliage and made their occasional very loud, high-pitched meow like call.

To our left is a statue of the elephant god Ganesha (also called Ganapathi). Hindu tradition states that Ganesha is a god of wisdom, success and good luck. He is also the giver of different types of favours and is the remover of obstacles. Most Hindus also worship Ganesha before starting any new project, and it is traditional to chant first to Ganesha when entering a temple.

We stop before the deity, and I say the mantra 'Om Gam Ganapataye Namaha'. This mantra means we bow to the qualities of the divine represented by Ganesha. The mantra wards off all the negativities from one's life before beginning any work, and when entering a temple, clear any negativity and resistance within ourselves. Many westerners struggle with the idea of bowing to an elephant-headed idol. However, when you see it as a symbolic act of clearing our resistance to divine knowledge, the process becomes a lot easier.

We then enter the main temple area and offer our respects to a statue of Saraswathi, the goddess of knowledge and Akanda Jyothi (divine flame) inside the Saraswathi Mantapam. We then head to Sri Kalyana Subramanya Temple (Lord Murugan) and Sri Shirdi Sai Baba Temple. After this, we climb down the stairs to enter the Saraswathi Mantapam and then exit to offer prayers at the Sri Kaala Bhairava Temple. Once this is done, we visit the Guru Peedam and offer respects to Sri Dakshinamoorthy (the aspect of the Hindu god Shiva as a guru).

There is a lot to take in in all of these areas. To get to the Sri Kalyana Subramanya Temple, you ascend an eighteen runged ornate brass staircase that becomes red-hot in the Indian sun and is an interesting challenge to us barefooted pilgrims. The presiding deity here is Sri Kalyana Subrahmanya. I learned later that this place is a particularly auspicious place to put your horoscope at the feet of Lord Subrahmanya. People will do this on a full moon day and come back after 40 days to collect the horoscope. This pooja is said to trigger happy events for anyone that does this.

Ash and I then walk around the small cylindrical shaped temple at the top of the stairs. We circumnavigate it three times, paying homage to the gods Tiruchendur, Palani, Swami Malai, Thiruthani, and Pazhamudhircholai and eventually enter the Sri Shirdi Sai Baba Temple.

Sri Shirdi Sai Baba (1838—October 15, 1918) is the first incarnation of Sathya Sai Baba. There is no temple dedicated to Sathya Sai Baba though I noticed a large painting of him on the side of the main temple complex. As I have already mentioned, many followers of Sharanana Baba are also followers of Sathya Sai Baba, who died on 24 April 2011. Temples to Sri Shridi Sai Baba are rare in Kerala.

The temple priest was on duty and was giving me a ferocious look.

"Put your camera away, Craig," said Ash. "You are not supposed to film in here."

Another bungle, but the priest was fine as soon as I apologised and invited me to film whatever I wanted. He spent some time explaining the various things shown in the temple, including a collection of statues, possessions and pictures that Sharavana Baba had used as a boy and a young man.

In the centre of the temple is an idol of Shirdi Sai Baba and to the right is an impressive 6-foot Lingam made of Copper that is dedicated to Lord Shiva. Copper is a holy metal and radiates energy.

On the left, as you enter, is also a shrine to Maha Avatar Babaji, the miraculous yogi who was the guru of Lahiri Mahasaya and is described in Autobiography of a Yogi by Yogananda.

Siddhars

What most caught my attention was the back of the temple where there were idols to what I recognized as the 18 Siddhars, who are responsible for developing science, mathematics, medicine, astronomy, astrology, Yoga, Philosophy, Metaphysics, creativity and literature. The 18 Siddhars lived for hundreds and, in some cases, thousands of years. Some are still said to be living in the Himalayas and remote areas of Southern India.

I am particularly attracted to these as it is the 18 Siddhars under the leadership of Sri Agastya who wrote the Naadi oracles that changed the course of my life radically. Agastya initiated many Siddhas, including our kriya guru Babaji. He was initiated directly by Lord Shiva himself, and his works include medicine, Kaya Kalpa, Tamil grammar and yoga. The miraculous jiva naadi of Agastya told me to take my seriously ill grandson to see Sharavana Baba – the story you read at the start of this book.

Our journey through the temple area ends at the Sri Dakshinamoorthy Temple, which is in effect a large hall with an idol of Sri Dakshinamoorthy set in an alcove at one end. This place is used every day for a spectacular pooja using lamps. The back of the hall opens out to the plantations.

"Sri Dakshinamoorthy is the Adi Guru, the union of Shaiva and Vaishnava energies, worshipped for Wisdom and to attain dispassionate detachment," said Ash. "Let's now spend some time in meditation here. This area is the most energy-rich place on the ashram, and meditating at this spot helps to accelerate spiritual development."

As we sat in meditation, my mind focused on the meaning of Sri Dakshinamoorthy as the Adi Guru. After all, I am here for the Maha Shivratri, so it would be good spiritual practice to get to the bottom of who Shiva is. For us, westerners – and I think for many Indians too – the Hindu culture can be overwhelming with its many ideas.

Many people take away a very superficial understanding of the Hindu culture. In yoga clubs, for example, the teachings can be simple and self-evident. Apart from the whacky stuff and gym-style yoga classes, most yogic teachings originate in the instructions of Patanjali, but the transformative effects of poojas, the magical power of mantras, the worship of gods and goddesses and so on are usually overlooked.

On one level, the teachings show us how to live well and have a healthy and happy life, but there are also stories of people who have used the systems to catapult their consciousness into the furthest frontiers of existence. The 18 Siddhars, for example, displayed extraordinary spiritual powers that defy the imagination. These were once men but somehow became supermen. Sri Shirdi Sai Baba did likewise, as did his next incarnation in the form of Sathya Sai Baba, whose materialization of Vibhuti ash I saw at close quarters.

It seems that the more you dig and uncover the ancient Indian culture, the more you find, and the process seems to go on endlessly. It's hard to get to the bottom of it and nail it down, and I've decided that it is impossible to understand by using conventional study. You have to dive in.

Shiva is a figure that I at first found hard to understand. I have felt an incredible magnetism from the thought of Shiva. On one occasion, when I first took a serious interest in learning the deeper aspects of yoga, I had a compelling vision of Shiva. I saw his blue-skinned form sitting in Padmasana on my yoga mat in front of me. As I opened my eyes from meditation for a short moment, I was shocked to see him there. The vision was wholly unexpected and as clear as day.

At that time, I had no idea that Shiva was the god of yogis. This blue figure is Shiva in the form known as the Adi Guru or Adi Yogi. In this temple where I now sat, they call him Sri Dakshinamoorthy.

Shiva is a part of the Trimurti, a triad of the three most powerful Hindu gods. Brahma is the creator, Vishnu is the preserver, and Shiva is the destroyer. Shiva also has a human form as the first Guru or the Adi Guru. The myths say that when he attained Self-realisation, he became ecstatic and danced over the mountains or sat as still as a corpse. He alternated between moments of stillness and bouts of wild dancing. He was a man, a god and also the whole of existence.

Shiva can be the Absolute, the Brahman and the spirit of all sentient beings. The Absolute is, therefore, the first guru. Alternatively, Adi yogi may have been a real man who lived 15,000 years ago and was the first to attain enlightenment. In the stories from the Puranas, he is married to a woman called Parvathi, who gave birth to two yogis called Skanda and Ganesha.

Whether these stories are based on actual events or are metaphorical myths is a topic for debate. Some say that Adiyogi is the same being as Dakshinamoorthy, who in the stories sends eight rishis to different parts of the world to spread spiritual knowledge. Some say that Adiyogi was a yogi called Nandinatha who lived in mount Kailash and was the guru of Patanjali. Others say that the word 'Shiva' means 'auspicious' and can therefore be applied to many gods. In the Vedas, it is sometimes used as an adjective. Historians tell us that Shiva developed from Rudra, a fierce storm god worshipped in the Indus Valley during the Vedic period.

I sat contemplating these ideas. Does it matter who is who or what god is what? Intellectual knowledge can be a distraction from a direct spiritual experience. In my heart, I feel that in ancient days superhuman people walked the earth. Perhaps they were people from other dimensions or other planets or, more likely, humans who had attained such a state of spiritual awareness that the rest of us can't understand. None of it really matters. What is essential is our enlightenment and spiritual development. These idols connect us to that part within ourselves that already knows the highest truth. We must become Shiva.

"One more temple to visit," said Ash when he saw me finish my 'meditation'. "the Sri Naaga Kshethra Temple is a short walk from here."

We walked barefoot along a dirt track through a plantation area to a small temple surrounded by trees. It is a simple open-roofed structure built on a brick base on an elevated plane with steps leading up to the top. As we ascended the steps, I could feel the peace of the place. It had a wet earthy smell and was cool from the overhang of the trees. This place was the most tranquil area of the ashram.

It was similar in many ways to the Naaga shrine I had visited in the jungle yesterday. In the centre is a large dark stone area housing the Nagga snake gods Sri Rahu and Sri Kethu. The images and stone surround was stained yellow from turmeric used in Poojas. As I explained earlier, the snake gods are the protectors of planet earth, and they are responsible for health, wisdom, family development, and spiritual evolution.

The snake Gods, Sri Rahu and Sri Ketu, are the two planets in the solar system, renowned for energy and wisdom. Most temples in South India have a special place for the snake Gods and are revered with utmost devotion.

We paid our respects to the gods and, as is the tradition in India, walked around the temple's perimeter three times.

Aghori Yogis

Next to the Sri Naaga Kshethra Temple is a large rectangular area cut into the earth to a depth of about 10 feet. In the corner is a rocky area that, at certain times of the year, becomes a spring that will fill the pit with water for various rituals involving bathing. For now, the area was dry and is primarily used for poojas involving fire and incense and a lot of dancing and singing.

I sat with Ash on the stone steps that descend into the pit. Here we could contemplate the surrounding canopy of trees, listen to the squawks of strange birds and chat about the spiritual power of this mysterious place. Fingers of light were reaching through the foliage and casting a beautiful golden display through the rising incense burners that were quietly draping the area in swirling patterns of aromatic smoke. Somewhere nearby, a Brahmin was chanting a mantra that I did not understand.

I had heard Sharavana Baba say that this place was where the Aghori yogis of old used to gather in a time when this place was a dense forest. I asked Ash if he knew anything more about this.

"As far as I understand things," says Ash "Swami made this area so that the Aghori yogis in various forms could visit this place and participate in various Indian festivals."

"What I know of the Aghori is that they are extreme ascetics," I reply. "There are stories of them eating human flesh and living in graveyards and cremation grounds. When I went to Varanasi, I saw some of them. One caught my attention, and he scared the living daylights out of me when he looked me in the eye."

"Yes, they will literally scare you to death," replied Ash "but this is not what its' really about."

"I understand it as a path where you take things to such an extreme that life is no longer worth living," I reply. "The person realises it's better to let go of the world and move on to a higher state. It's like using the horror of death as the fuel to push you towards non-attachment."

"What you've described to me is like escapism from life," continued Ash. "I see it as more to do with acceptance of everything. For example, we see vomit as a bad thing because it is associated with illness and sickness, but it is part of our biological identity, so it should not repulse us.

"The true Agora train for many years and are extremely rare. Others just use it as an excuse to smoke a chillum and get stoned. It's disrespectful to the objectives of the true Aghori."

"So, what is the objective of the true Aghori yogis?" I ask. "And what avenues do they go down?"

"The objective of all aspects of Hinduism is the realisation we are divine. The Aghoris then go further and harness those energies to use them for specific purposes," replies Ash. "Those avenues being whatever you will discover in your life should you go down them."

"So it is an acceptance of everything," I say.

"All divine life, whatever your religious or cultural background be it Buddhist, Islamic, Sikhism or Christian, the objective as quoted in the true scriptures has always been enlightenment," says Ash. "However, a paradox is that our apparent ignorance comes into this and fights with us on this inward journey.

"It feels like our ignorance - which can be described as the false belief that we are separate from one another due to egoic conditioning - creates an opposing force to our attainment of reality and prevents us from coming closer to the divine.

"That is at the heart of Advaita: the understanding and recognition that all is one. It means going beyond ignorance through introspection and investigation until the truth reveals itself to us.

"So anyone who practices under the guise of Aghori, without fully comprehending the importance of this path, enters another cycle of escapism. This delusion is like a trap that gradually moves one away from the divine instead of closer to the truth.

"The whole purpose of any religious or cultural divine practice is to come out of our ignorance so that we realize who we are."

The left-hand Tantric path of the Aghoris works at the limits of social taboo. It is a path not for the faint-hearted that requires a fearless attitude and an uncompromising dedication to the goal of transcendence and the self's identity with the absolute. Their practices are very far removed from orthodox Hinduism and involve rites. They smear cremation ashes on their bodies and use bones from human corpses to craft kapalas (skull cups) and jewellery. Their rituals sometimes include cannibalism, eating excrement and drinking urine from human skulls.

The Aghoris venerate the fierce manifestation of Lord Shiva represented in black-skinned god Kala Bhairava. He has angry eyes shaped like lotus blossoms, fiery red hair and tiger's teeth. Around his neck is coiled a snake together with a dreadful garland of human skulls. Kala Bhairava is not a particularly cheery figure of worship.

The name Kala Bhairava is familiar to me in my first ever Naadi reading; the rishi tells me that this was my adopted name in a previous incarnation. I had been the priest in charge of the temple but had had a ferocious temper and would throw people out at the slightest transgression. Considering the characteristics of the god, I must have had one hell of a temper.

Unlike Patanjali, who sees them as a distraction from the goal of Samadhi, the Aghori yogis value Siddhis powers (supernatural powers) as a means to liberation. They believe that wisely using Siddhis can accelerate a person's spiritual evolution.

As well as the familiar psychic gifts of clairvoyance and telepathy, the Agori yogis strive for superpowers to overcome the material world. Kaya Siddhi, for example, is the power to extend one's life indefinitely utilizing the 'Immortal body'. If an Aghori develops the Maya Siddhi, he gains control over the material world. Herbs and minerals are taken at astrologically auspicious times to trigger these powers. They also use Mantra, Yantra and Tantra in their quest towards supernatural powers and immortality. Some Aghori live in graveyards and charnel grounds to entrap spirits and force them to perform tasks.

The Aghoris will notice when his Prana or life force begins to flow out of his body and knows that this is a sign of his impending death within six months. During this period, Aghoris will deliberately leave their bodies and enter the bodies of corpses. They will animate the corpse and take them over and making them live for as long as they please. When the possessed body is of no more use, they will change bodies again.

Happiness for enlightenment?

The Aghori's path is a rugged and unremitting path to

enlightenment, and its harsh demands are far from the self-indulgent body worshipping yoga we see in the West. Similarly, western spirituality has become shallow and insipid. On Facebook and other social media, we see well-meaning fools share quotations and misquotations of spiritual masters so that they can look wise to their friends. A constant stream of posts bombards us by people trying to impress, so great words sink into this amalgam of gooey insignificance. A single phrase that could be a key to spiritual transformation is lost on the endless scroll of attention-grabbing trivia. Because of this, contemporary people have a very shallow grasp of spirituality. Few today do the research and study necessary to gain spiritual clarity, and fewer still would consider taking on hardship as part of their spiritual path.

Our collective obsession with finding happiness is making many people ill. America's self-help industry is worth upward of $11 billion and promises many easy fixes that don't seem to work. Preoccupation with happiness may be taking us further from the goal we want to achieve. All the positive thinking and self-improvement is taking people nowhere as they set materialistic goals, and although for some this may bring temporary happiness, it is not permanent. Trying too hard is also a false path.

We are better off opening up to life, relaxing and accepting each moment no matter what it holds. When we seek happiness, we lose the spirit of acceptance that could be a way to happiness.

Today's view of 'happiness' is of the idea of personal happiness characterised by satisfaction with life and feeling positive rather than negative emotions.

Failing to appear happy is cause for concern. Western culture assumes that happiness is the most important value for guiding individuals' lives. And we search for it wherever we can – primarily in an endless quest for material and emotional satisfaction found in the objective world. We seek happiness outside of ourselves, but in reality, we are seeking distraction from our dissatisfaction.

There are also individuals, cultures and religions that appear to be adverse to happiness and make a virtue out of being miserable. Could it be that some people have a 'fear of happiness' and use religion to avoid situations that elicit happiness. The fear in these types is that happiness tends to cause or be followed by sadness. Why go up when you have to go down again? Using this logic, some depressed people are fearful of being happy. Happiness leads to unhappiness, they say, and this outweighs the benefits of being happy.

Medieval Christianity played into this downward spiral with its pleasure taboos that still hold some influence today. Happiness in the form of material success, positivity, and merriment was the way to damnation. These terrible things would draw the Christian away from God. And we can find similar unfortunate ideas in other Middle Eastern religions. Prophet Muhammad says that "were you to know what I know, you would laugh little and weep much" and "avoid much laughter, for much laughter deadens the heart." (Quran, 5:87). Some artists, too, have commented that their work is enhanced by suffering and unhappiness.

Perhaps the point is that extremes of euphoria and depression are the wrong path and that religion can stabilise our way. Life denying miserableness cannot, in my opinion, be the course to enlightenment. Total rejection of worldly things may be suitable for a special few, such as the Aghoris, but happiness lights our way to the truth for most people. The Buddha followed the course of the extreme renunciate, but he concluded that the middle way is the surest path. Happiness is achieved when a person directly understands the true nature of reality unmodified by what we try to superimpose upon it. He realized that 'our life is the creation of our mind'.

One view of happiness then is that it is dependent on how we see things. The naturally miserable person will seek out reasons to be unhappy and usually likes to make everyone else's lives miserable. The weak person laments that the world is against them and that others have more than they do, whereas the happy soul sees support everywhere and rejoices in the success of others.

Happiness takes hard work. It comes partly through inner discipline and by training ourselves to drop afflictive emotions that poison the mind. Through spiritual work, we can eradicate ignorance and come to understand that happiness or otherwise is of our own making. William Shakespeare summed this idea up perfects in Hamlet with the words, "There is nothing either good or bad, but thinking makes it so."

As I sat on the steps to the Aghori pits with Ash and watched the last smoke from the incense burners entwine a course through the parallel rays of golden sunshine, I thought about how hard it is to break our attachment to this world and move like this whispy smoke into the next. My task as a medium has been the opposite of the Aghori. I aim to free people from the fear of death and know that life continues into other worlds and other lives until we merge again with the ineffable oneness of creation. Yet what I suggest is a long upwardly spiralling path filled with the repeating pain of attachment, the grief of loss and the joy of reunion. The Aghori bypass all of this. They are fearless and embrace all that an average person rejects.

The naadis had told me that my name in a former life had been Kala Bhairava, and I pondered whether I had once followed a harsh and non-compromising spiritual path. Probably not. If I struggle with a brand new bed, I don't know how I'd cope with sleeping in a graveyard. It also strikes me as a dangerously drastic path to liberation. I'm sure it's more refreshing and practical than the indulgent touch/feely insipid western yoga that has taken the stage today. Nonetheless, the courageous Agori yogi's approach is a slippery path that could equally bring karmic consequences that may lengthen the way to salvation.

It's not one for me. I'm not sure if I would like an immortal physical life if it entails jumping from corpse to corpse and spending centuries drinking vomit from sculls. I can think of better things to do.

"Shall we get lunch now?" asked Ash.

"Yes, sure." It had to be better than what I was consuming in my imagination.

Time to Be

As we waited for our turn to get the food, I thought about how nice it is to slow down to a different life pace. It is a rare treat to sit and talk and listen to the world's sounds around us or have the time to contemplate the trees' colours and shapes. The journey and the ever-new culture shock that is India was still resonating in the background of my consciousness. Now the impressions of the trip and the clamour of my mind faded into the silence of the ashram.

When we were babies, we lived entirely in the present. Our experience was mostly at rest and only occasionally interrupted by new external stimuli. As children, our understanding of time changed as we settled into routines that seemed to be eternal. But as our sense of self arose and the world crammed in, time speeded up. The pace gathers throughout our lives until most of us discover that we have no time left. Soon we are in our sixties, seventies and eighties, and in no time at all, time is gone.

Time is intimately connected with our attention. Time can go fast or slow or seem to stop, but time leaks away when our attention is lost. Few of us train our attention or discipline the restless mind. How many of us can sit quietly doing nothing, observe the breath or watch the rise and fall of thoughts on the screen of our attention? It was a challenging task in past ages, but now, our attention is ambushed like never before. We fidget our way through life, multitask ourselves into traumas and wonder why we feel so much unease. We are forever somewhere else and lose touch with the precious now. Happiness exists only in the present moment, and working with joy in our heart – even if we fake it – will centre our being in the now.

How we apply ourselves to life and the work at hand determines how quickly and how much ease we complete our goals. If we add the ingredient of happiness to all we do, all sorts of things are possible. "When we work with a heavy heart and gloomy condition, there will not be any prosperity," says Sharavana in one of his discourses. "But, if you work with happiness, you will become prosperous. Live with happiness. Then only we can pass happiness to all those who come to us."

Even the holy men and priests carry mobile phones. The endless mind-numbing distractions of the internet have captured everyone's souls it seems. We imprison ourselves in distractions – a forever 'play again' button that leaves no room for contemplation or a free flow of thought. Our attention has gone, and with it, time dies. How can we ever find happiness if we lose touch with the present moment? Happiness is not found in the past or the future. Happiness has to be here and now.

At the ashram, I have time. Here I can even think about time. Perhaps time can go backwards, forwards, speed up, stand still or go up and sideways. Could it be that the laws of physics may allow time to exist in different forms? Our ancestors must have experienced time if a completely different way from us today. They lived in a perpetual present, whereas we live forever, rushing to the future. Today's world would be incomprehensible to them. And how will our experience of time change with the evolution of human consciousness?

My revelry is interrupted by the vibration of my mobile phone in my pocket. It's a text message from Jane: "Happy Valentine's Day."

Note to self: I really must pay more attention.

The Food

Jane always says that I remember where we have been by what I have eaten. The food here takes some getting used to if you were raised in a restaurateurs family like me. I had seen the kitchens on the floor below where we now sat down to eat. It had mud floors with huge fire pits atop, which sat enormous caldrons. An English health inspector would have had a coronary if he'd seen all this. Ash had told me earlier that the caldrons that were big enough to boil a man in had been donated by Krishna, our hero from London who had rescued us from the perils of a night on the airport floor.

My mind cast back to when my family owned an American style restaurant in the UK that they'd modelled on the Hard Rock Café in London. We'd had our hygiene problems when a pet shop selling grain had opened next door to our restaurant. It attracted mice, so occasionally, one managed to make it through to our premises.

I can still remember my mother's poker face when a customer cried, "Aghhhh, it's a rat; it's a rat!" My mother didn't blink. "No, we don't have any mice here. There's not a chance we employ specialist services to ensure that this can never happen." She continued with her refusals with the skill of a spy trained to beat a lie detector.

It was amazing how my mother could simply use

denial to convince everyone that mice could not possibly exist. Even I was convinced yet I'd seen it with my own eyes. It was like a scene from the sitcom Faulty Towers with John Cleese.

Fortunately, our family's restaurant problems were solved when the adjoining grain store closed and was replaced by undertakers. Our clients could now feel reassured that no mice were in range but that dead bodies were being prepared for burial on the other side of the wall.

By Indian standards, the hygiene and the quality of the food at the ashram were excellent. Ash and Alison reassured me that they had visited the ashram on many occasions and had never been sick. Similarly, there were many London visitors, and it was infrequent for people to get stomach problems. And I can now vouch for that.

The food itself was, however, very bland, consisting mainly of rice. I am used to quite rich and savoury food, so it took a lot of adjusting. I am not a vegetarian, so it was a far cry from my regular diet, but I have to admit that my digestion was better than it's ever been. The food is plain and simple, and the water, coloured slightly brown by the iron in the soil, can be drunk without using sterilisation tablets.

After reading this book, you can travel there with confidence if you decide you'd like to visit the ashram. You are unlikely to get sick even if you are a fat pink and pampered westerner like me.

Sharavana makes a prophecy

Later that day, we ended up back at the steps where we had sat talking by the Sri Naaga Kshethra Temple. Sharavana had conducted a pooja to the snake gods and then fell into a trance. He began moaning and calling out in Malayalam. His face transformed, and he now looked very different from the chubby-faced Sharavana Baba that I knew. He appeared thinner and had a strange narrow look to his face – a little like a snake perhaps?

I had witnessed transfiguration within spiritualism and had occasionally exhibited this myself during my trance circles. In spiritualist circles, the medium goes into a trance and sometimes, a light veil of ectoplasm appears over the mediums face that takes the form of the faces of people we may know in the spirit world. The spirits of people we know will then talk through the medium to give messages from the other world. The communicating spirit provides facts about their former life on earth that verify its reality. This evidence of survival stands to prove that it is the dead loved one communicating. Transfiguration will only happen in very dark conditions as the ectoplasm is extremely sensitive to light.

From what I could see through the crowd pushing towards him, Sharavana was in a sudden and deep trance. This is very different from the trance states I had seen and experienced within Spiritualism. To me, it was reminiscent of the shamanistic trances of Tibetan Buddhism and tribal societies in which an animal, nature spirit or god will speak through the medium.

Sharavana called out in Malayalam as some of his

closest devotees held up his shivering body. I could not understand him, of course, but his tone was disturbing. Fortunately, a person near to me told me that the gods were talking through Sharavana.

"He is saying that this coronavirus will soon spread around the world," said the person beside me. "This will not be the only pandemic. There will be two more after this one in the future."

CHAPTER 19

Meeting and Darshan

Ashram life follows a slow and steady rhythm. There is no pressure, or need, to participate in everything that is going on. You can take your time and join in whatever draws you. At 5:30 am, activities begin with a Homa (also spelt Homan and sometimes called a Yajna). Homa is Sanskrit for a ritual, wherein an oblation or any religious offering is made into a sacred fire. For the Maha Shivaratri, a gigantic Homa will be lit. For now, the brick-built Homa was under construction in readiness for the final stages of the activities.

I could see the priests plastering the six fook high edifice with wet cow dung as I entered the Temple complex and sat to listen to a talk by Sharanana. Fortunately, there was someone there to translate, but his English was hard to understand, and I could only grab a few precious snippets of wisdom from the talk. He spoke about the importance of family, service to one another, the biological mother, the guru and the divine mother. Then Sharavana summarized in English:

"In all activities, we need to remember mother, father, guru and God. Father, mother, guru and God, they are all the same. All activities can be grace. Happiness is divine. Remember all the time. Life is not an illusion. Life is good. Life is beauty. Life is fun. Life is blissful. Life is divine."

He concluded with a prayer to the nine planets and explained that it is imperative to pray to the Navagraha. Sharahana holds a flame from camphor oil in his palm as he says the prayer. It looks as if the fire comes directly from his hands, and it is surprising how he never seems to get any burns from this ritual.

There are many prayers, poojas' talks, and festivities thought the days and nights, but the most cherished moments are when you get to talk with Sahravana face to face. Once a day after these talks, there is a chance when we queue for the guru's 'darshan'. Everyone gets just a few minutes with the swami, but it is incredible how much he can communicate in such a short time.

Big Book

I come to the front of the line and get my chance to be with swami for a few moments. He is pleased to see me and takes hold of my hand as we speak together.

"I have an idea for the title of my book," I say. "What do you think of the title 'Be Happy'?"

"Yes, yes, good title. Now let's make it a BIG book!" said swami as his eyes widened, emphasizing the word 'big'.

We both burst into laughter. The two of us knew right from the start when, in London, he asked me to India to write a 'little, little, book' that this was never going to happen. His plan was for me to write a complete book.

"I knew you'd trap me like this," I said between giggles.

It's a strange thing that no matter what one's mood or intentions, when you approach Sharavana, it all just evaporates, and you find yourself in a silly, cheerful and compliant mood.

"Nice big book," he repeated with the look of a puppy dog across his face.

"Of course," I replied as I surrendered to the inevitable. "It's all a Lila"

At an earlier meeting in England, swami had taken me aside and said that it is vital that people worship their ancestors. He said that people nowadays had forgotten about these necessary poojas and that maybe I could remind them. When I was planning the book title, I wondered whether I should include references to my work as a medium in the book. Swami knew that I was a medium, but I did not vocalise my thoughts.

"Any activity to the ancestors brings blessing," he said as he read my mind. "It brings happiness and divine grace. All ancestors are also the guru and divine. Happiness increases in your life."

Feeding the Dead

Sometime later, when I was back in England, my thoughts returned to this moment whilst I was doing a mediumistic reading for someone over the telephone. The caller was from India, and they were asking me to communicate with their father in the spirit. I couldn't 'hear' the spirit communicator's name on this occasion, but I gave them lots of information that proved to them that this was their father speaking from the other side of life.

I felt the spirit move close to me, and I could feel him pushing food into my mouth. I'd never had this happen when making a spirit link, and I expressed my feelings to my client.

"Your father is feeding me food," I said. "What does this mean?"

She explained that she had yesterday commemorated the dead with food. I learned that many Hindus feed large numbers of people to mark the end of mourning. The formal rites include offerings for the soul's passage from being a ghost to becoming an ancestor. Rice or flour balls - known as pindas - are offered to heaven. Some castes leave these pindas outside and hope that a crow will eat it. This is an auspicious sign that the ghost has become an ancestor (pitr).

I felt that the lady's father in spirit was grateful for the poojas and rituals she had been doing on his behalf. I agree that our thoughts and feelings will reach past the veil and reach those we love on the spirit side. Perhaps it is not so much the important details of the rituals but the feelings behind them that count. Love can cross any barrier, even the border between life and death.

Unfortunately, the time I get to speak to Sharavana is very brief. He has crowds of people queueing to see him, so I have to snatch a few words from him whenever we get the chance. He is fully aware that I am writing a book, and I notice that sometimes he includes answers to my questions in his public addresses.

I'd been thinking about chance, luck and coincidences and how our thoughts fly from us to attract good or bad things into our lives. Suddenly swami changed the subject of what he was talking about, looked at me and said: "After we chant, we awaken the senses. Worship is inside. Service is outside. If the worship inside is perfect, then the outside world becomes perfect. Worship first, and all blessings come. Thoughts, words and actions all increase the divine power within you. Live by divine power."

Most of the activities that happen on the ashram are worship in some form or other. For many of the visiting westerners I spoke to, the pageant and ritual can be overwhelming. I asked one of the visiting devotees from London and who'd come from a traditional Hindu background. "I can assure you," he quipped "that we find it just as much as a culture shock as you do!"

From the moment Sharavana wakes up, he seems to be forever lighting camphor oils, sprinkling turmeric and throwing flowers at altars. Many of these ceremonies point to complex metaphysical concepts and echo the early Dravidian religion that constituted a non-Vedic form of Hinduism.

Sometimes sitting on the hard floors for long hours of pujas and untranslated discourses can be pretty strained. Your legs go numb, the lower back nags with aches, and the attention wanders. However, if you are open and attentive, you realize that Swami directly instructs us with every word and action. He is acutely aware of every thought of everyone in the vicinity. For example, I was sitting with eyes closed and my head filled with monkey-mind ideas moaning about how I could be somewhere else or whether all this was just a money-making con and so on.

I felt someone gently patting my back. All the negative thoughts evaporated, and I experienced a feeling of great inner peace. I looked around to see swami crouched by me, patting my back and beaming at me with a shining smile. I don't think my face had given anything away about my thoughts, but he had somehow picked up on my internal conflict.

"Hold your lamps," he said to everyone. "Pray for inner peace, pray for world peace. Pray for peace, happiness, health and wealth for everyone you love." During my stay at the ashram, I noticed that whatever was happening inside my head was often expressed in the words spoken by Sharavana.

At the close of that afternoon's events, I briefly spoke with him at darshan. As I had decided that the book title should be 'Be Happy', I'd better understand what happiness is. So I asked.

"Swami, what is happiness?"

"Happiness is awakening inside. Inside all is light. Inside all is strength. Inside all is happiness. Happiness is living from the inside."

He then breaks into a beaming smile and gives a thumbs up with both hands. I loved his answer. It was simple yet profound, and his face bore witness to its reality.

Down by the Riverside

The ashram runs at a slow and peaceful pace with the occasional intermission of extraordinary and hectic events. Although there is a set schedule for the events leading up to Maha Shivaratri, swami likes to announce unexpected program changes.

"Mr Craig, you must buy some new Indian clothes as you are to take a bath at the river," a devotee told me. "You need these for wearing in the river."

I had no idea what he was talking about, but I found out when I bumped into Alison and Ash further along the road. I could see that they were both very excited. They told me that swami had announced that we are all to go to the river tonight, and all the men – me included - will be bathing in the river.

"You will need Indian clothes for this," insisted Alison, "a white top and Dhoti like Ash is wearing now. If you leave now and walk down the road to the village, you'll be able to catch the store and buy everything you need. This event will be an all-nighter, so grab something to eat, have a nap until 3:00 am when we will all meet at the ashram gate."

Alison noted the expression on my face. "No, no, no, this is going to be a massively important experience," she said as she shook my arm. "It's a once in a lifetime opportunity!"

I had seen people bathing in the rivers on the way to the ashram and mused about how filthy it all looked and how lucky I was that I didn't have to drink, defecate and bathe in the same river. I also remembered the warning words the vaccination nurse gave before leaving about how one has to be very careful in rural India and never go near the rivers or other dirty places. My mind was filled with images of leeches, parasitical snails, water snakes, Dengue fever, Buruli Ulcers, Chagas Disease, Cysticercosis…

"I'd better get moving then," I said.

The sun plunged below the horizon as I left the ashram gates, and soon it was pitch black. The road ahead was treacherous with no pavement, but lots of open manholes, uncovered drains, slippery paths, exposed steel shards and as much rotting trash as you could ever wish for. I negotiated it all in my flimsy sandals as the headlights of overloaded lorries and lunatic drivers hurtled towards me out of the darkness.

I passed bare dilapidated shops, cows grazing on the trash and saw people sleeping under carts. Then like a luminous magical oasis in a dark desert, I saw the store. It shone like a beacon of hope and was so out of place. It has pristine marble floors, a shiny glass frontage with elaborate window décor and a smartly uniformed greeter who would look after your shoes while you entered the building. It felt like I had stumbled upon Harrods.

I counted six salespeople who helped me make my purchases and who fussed over me as if I was the maharaja come to town. I bought some smart new Indian clothes for myself and managed to get Jane her yellow sari and a few more high-quality dresses, and it all cost next to nothing. As I stepped from the polished marble and back onto the dirt street, I thought about how surreal it was to be buying beautiful clothes and then wearing them in the muddy river. Some may marvel at my new outfit or maybe marvel at my stupidity.

I got back to my room at the ashram late and slept

poorly. A silly woman in a room nearby had decided to spend the night chanting peace mantras. I awoke to feel grumpy and ready to murder someone. I showered and dressed and made it to the pick-up point in the early hours and just in time to catch the last of the night's mosquitoes.

The man who sat next to me on the bus told me about the snake house that was just visible as we drove away from the ashram. He explained that a family had once lived in the house, but snakes moved in, and the family moved out. I asked him to explain why they didn't just remove the snakes.

"This land originally belonged to the snakes," he said. "Now we lock the house, and it is full of baby snakes. The snakes are a very auspicious sign of a blessing from Shiva. The house belongs to the snakes now. It has become a sacred place."

"So why are the snake and the Naga worship so important?" I asked.

"Think of it as removing the poison from life," he replied. "Some situations and some people are full of poison. We, too, can be full of poison. Shiva and the snakes help us remove the poison."

The bus dropped all of us men in the middle of the jungle. The women would follow later but what lay ahead was a ceremony for men only. It was still night, and I was barefoot, and as the colossal moon peeped through the jungle canopy, I marvelled at how remote this all was from my everyday life. It was a primordial place, and what we were about to do reached back to the earliest times. This strange setting was the world of archaic man, a pre-logical world that existed before the dawn of rampant rationality and anxiety that blights the modern soul. In the primaeval world, the senses heighten, and for a short time, we regain our connection with the mysterious. This place is the world of sorcerers, dreams, spirits and talking trees.

My revelry was broken by a loud voice directed at a man nearby. "Don't sit on the woodpile! That is where the snakes hide during the night." The man leapt to his feet like a jack-in-the-box.

My new friend from the bus resumed our discussion about snakes. "Swami protects us from snakes in the ashram but only to 7:00 pm. After this, they roam free. It is their land. We must leave even the naga temple to them. Here too, swami will protect us from snakes."

"I have heard that in ancient times there was a war between men and snakes," I say.

"Yes, this took place tens of thousands of years ago. In the past, snakes were huge, and men were giants too. Men won the battle with the snakes."

I found it fascinating that so many of the Malayali people I had met on this journey had such a reverence for snakes. Of course, many cultures regarded snakes as immortal because they appeared to be reincarnated from themselves when they sloughed their skins. Also, the behaviour of snakes and their unblinking, lidless eyes imply intelligence and awareness and that they have a thought process that is alien to humans. Nonetheless, it is odd that so many cultures put such significance on the snake. It strikes me that maybe these beliefs hark to a time when strange things happened that still have echoes in our mythologies and religions.

Our discussion was interrupted when two pink

vehicles arrived that – to me, a least – looked like two ice-cream vans. Disappointingly it turns out that these are the ashram vehicles bringing the pooja materials used in the river ceremonies. We next form a line and wind our way along the dirt path that leads through to the jungle and to the river. Every step reveals something sharp, but thoughts of discomfort fade as the dark mystery and awe of the world ahead envelopes us.

At the end of the trail, we came to a muddy bank where the grey Kunthipuzha river was snaking slowly under the moonlight. The men from the 'ice cream vans' had got there ahead of us and had set up some lights and laid out hundreds of pots. These brass pots with a large base and mouth just big enough to hold a coconut are the Kalasa pots used in many poojas in the temples. They are to be filled with river water and later adorned with coconut and mango leaves. The arrangement is called Purna-Kalasha and is considered a symbol of abundance and "source of life" in the Vedas. It is believed to contain amrita, the elixir of life, and is seen as a symbol of abundance, wisdom, and immortality.

We are all given a pot to carry. It is our job to take in tonto the river and then carry it back to the ashram's temple areas.

As I'm looking at all this, swami arrives and, in a loud booming voice, chants, "Arohara!" We all respond with "Arohara!" and continue chanting as we follow Sharavana down to the riverside. I found out later that this chant is a shortened form of the phrase 'ara harO harA'. Its meaning is 'Oh God Almighty, please remove our sufferings and grant us salvation.'

Despite its weighty meaning, its sound is celebratory, like a call of joy. To me, it sounded reminiscent of the cheery Hawaiian call of Aloha!

Sharavana's eyes were sparkling, and he wore a broad smile as he initiated the chant. He was clearly enjoying it all, and the atmosphere was soon filled with a joyous vibration as we all joined in and marched towards the water. I have to say that religion in India is often fun. The chanting increases into whoops as we all follow swami into the river. He is wearing his best emerald green robes whilst the rest of us have removed our white shirts and wear just a Dhobi. Amongst all of this brown skin, I look somewhat like a pink beached whale.

"Arohara!" is shouted again, and from waste deep, we now all duck beneath the water until we are completely submerged. I had done something similar when I visited the Ganges, but the atmosphere here was electrifying. In India, water plays an integral part in many rituals and poojas. Water is revered as it represents physical and spiritual cleanliness and well-being. Through it, we strive to attain purity and avoid pollution. And, of course, as in Christianity, it also represents rebirth.

There is also a sense of connectedness when we all gather like this in a river. The water is a uniting element, and there's a sense of being spiritually connected with the guru. I'm not usually one for pageants and ceremonies, but I have to admit that the atmosphere of the river at night, the chanting and the presence of a holy man made the whole experience uniquely inspiring. I'd do it again, despite my concerns about leeches, dengue fever and the like.

Once we get out of the water, the 108 pots are

wrapped in leaves and flowers, and I take one to swami. He says to me, "This is to help the world," and then gives me a mantra that I must chant as I carry the pot back to the ashram. Everyone receives a different mantra which I realise is a single line each from the Sri Subrahmanya Ashtothram – the 108 names of Lord Skanda. (Also known as Kartikeya, Murugan and Subrahmanya.) Skanda and his many names are the deities of love and war. Most devotees of Kumara also revere members of his family: Parvati, Shiva, and Ganesha.

It's not often that I get the chance to stand in a steaming jungle with the brass pot on my head, barefooted and in drenched new clothes, but what a chance this was. The atmosphere was electric and mysterious, and I had a powerful feeling of being connected with ancient times. People had been doing this same ritual for millennia, way before the ancient greeks or far, far back into history. Here in India, the classical world was still alive, and I was part of it.

Moments later, we hear a distant chant of female voices move closer to us. The jungle is now alight with hundreds of lamps that the ashram women carry as they weave their way through the dark jungle. The light snakes its way towards us and finally separates into two lines of lights on either side of the jungle paths. We form a line and walk, with our pots atop our heads, back along the trail. The dark jungle hums with its natural sounds that merge with the resonance of mantras in a sea of tiny lights.

We walk and chant the 4-mile journey through the jungle and villages onto the main road and back to the ashram. As we enter the gates, the mantras get louder and louder as we approach the temple areas. One by one, the pots are taken from us by Sharavana and placed by gods and goddesses. Mine is the last one to be placed inside the final shrine. The mantras bust into a crescendo, and it all over.

It's a been long ceremony. I enter my room and lay on my bed with a head full of impossible thoughts and strange images. My mind shuts down, the early morning light dips to black, and I fall into a welcoming abyss of sleep.

CHAPTER 20

Strange Stories and Holy Fires

Tucked away near the entrance to the ashram is a small canteen café where visitors can get snacks and drinks. It's an excellent place to chill and reflect and meet other spiritual seekers. They also make a fantastic Masala Chai. I was here that I was able to chat with devotees and hear some of their remarkable stories about their miraculous experiences with Sharavana.

Many customers have fascinating stories to tell, and I recorded a few short chats with people who were willing to share their stories. I spoke with a 47-year-old man from Malaysia called Laksmi Kandon.

Laksmi: I met swami ten tears ago when he came to Malaysia, and the first thing he said was, 'You will meet your Sadguru at the age of 37'. I was shocked that he knew my exact age. Many swamis come to Malaysia, but few stay, which has not impressed me. 'This swami is here to stay', he told me as if reading my thoughts. And this is undoubtedly the case. From that day onward, I was hooked, and I now work with him every time he visits Malaysia.

Now he will stay at my house and stay with me for three weeks to a month, and we will do Seva with him. We also run programmes from the South to the North of Malaysia.

Craig: What is the most intriguing thing he has ever said to you?

Laksmi: When I was a young man of 17-year old, I used to take Kaudi and did other bad things, but Swamin knew everything I had done. I was a young man showing off a bit, and my family was not happy. He knew the entirety of my sins but also how I had now stopped. He knew the lot. He knew all about my family's worry about me and also how I had changed.

Craig: Has he ever healed anyone for you or predicted something about your future?

Laksmi: For me, the most important thing is that my life gets uplifted every time I see him. I was a poor man, but he kept improving my life. I keep thinking I am at my peak, but he keeps upgrading things for me, and life gets better and better. He says, 'I will upgrade you,' and then things miraculously change. He changed my status, job, prospects, many things and today; I am a company director. He helped me a lot. I am now dedicated to his feet.

One thing that I like about him is that he preaches about what is already there. He says there is nothing new. He says, 'I am not God; I am just the guru taking you there'. He tells me what I should do and explains the meaning of things and why I need to do what he suggests. His method of helping makes me feel very comfortable.

In life, you must have a guru. We say you have to have four things: Mata (mother), Pita (father), Guru(teacher) and Deva(God). Mother is the mother, the father is the father, and then you need to have a guru to reach God. From the age of 37, he became my guru. He takes me to see God.

Craig: Swami has a good sense of humour. Has anything funny ever happened?

Laksmi: I dream about him. Whenever he appears in my dream, he tells me what to do and gives me a prospectus for upcoming events I am to arrange. He gives me a list and tells me in detail what I need to do. All this happens before he announces that he is coming to Malaysia.

I then have to tell my friends what I have been notified of and prepare everything as per Sharavana's request.

Craig: So he makes all his travel arrangements through dreams with precise instructions.

Laksmi: Whenever he was coming to Malaysia, I dreamed of a prospectus. We then have to make arrangements and know what needs doing.

Craig: Fascinating

Laksmi: You also asked about healing. My mother had lung problems and problems breathing. She had to go to ICU seven times. At one time, my mother had been incubated and was in a complete coma. Swami told me not to worry. She will recover very soon as he will be with her.

My mother did recover and explained to me that she saw swami stand by her throughout her illness.

He was there in his spiritual form. Now she is fully healthy and lives in my house. She is now also a devotee. Whenever swami is in Malaysia, my mother will come to see him. All of my family are now devotees of swami.

So many people had stories to tell about miraculous events that surrounded Sharavana Baba. For example, Sharavana told one man on the ashram from Malaysia to make a veil and take it to a temple in Southern India. He had it made by a jeweller and put it in his suitcase and covered it well to be protected while travelling.

A few days later, he strongly felt that Sharavana asked him to open the suitcase. "Open the case. Open the case!" the inner voice said. He immediately stopped what he was doing and did as instructed. However, he was aghast to see the inside of the suitcase covered in large quantities of the Indian sacred ash called vibhuti. The materialized vibhuti he and others took as a sign of Sharavanah's divinity. They believe it connects Sharavana Baba to the famous Sai Baba of Shirdi, famed for similar materializations in his lifetime.

I was reminded of a story that Krishna – the man we stayed with in London – told me about when he went with Sharavana to bathe in the sea at the Tiruchendur Murugan temple located at the southern tip of India. At this holy location, it is customary to bathe in the ocean before entering the temple.

Krishna and a few others surrounded Sharavana in the water as he made a chant, and all sorts of holy objects manifested in the waves. Garlands of flowers, vibhuti, sacred threads, and Kumkum appeared out of the waves at Baba's behest.

Healing Powers

Some of the most startling stories people shared with me about Sharavana Baba were about his healing powers. For example, Jayalakshmi shared her story about the time she discovered a large lump on her breast.

Jayalakshmi: The lump was huge and hard. I am middle-aged, so the doctor told me that a biopsy must be taken as soon as possible. So arrangements were made for this, but before I was due to go, I heard that Sharavana Baba was visiting a place near me in Calicut.

So I went to Swami, and he said, "You have nothing to fear. Do everything the doctor tells you to do, and then you can good sleep at night." The next day things happened that prevented me from getting to the doctor. I was worried about what to do, so my husband and I decided that the best we could do was to go back to where we met swami and pray to him. So for a full day, we stayed with swami and prayed.

The next day I took a bath, and I noticed that it had become smaller and looser. This improvement was an encouragement, so I told my husband that we would pray to swami again today. After praying, I was able to talk to swami again at darshan, and he said to me that the lump had become smaller. I told him, yes, and he said, "Don't worry, swami is with you," and he handed me a pomegranate to eat. "You have to eat all of it," he said, "no sharing with others."

After this, everything went. The large, hard lump was completely gone.

Craig: So what did the doctor say?

Jayalakshmi: We didn't go back to the doctor. It

had just disappeared. Swami has told me, 'I will look after you,' so I put my faith in him, and it disappeared completely. I didn't need to go anywhere else.

Craig: When did this happen?

Jayalakshmi: It happened five years ago. From that point on, I decided to become a devotee of swami. Before this, I was a devotee of Mata Amritanandamayi (Amma). Now all of my family comes to see swami. I have a feeling that Swami knows everything. Every day, the feeling increases and our relationship with him grows closer and closer.

Craig: Who do you think he is?

Jayalakshmi: He is everything to me. He is all in one. You say mother, father, brother and close friend, but with Swami, it is a deep connection.

Many people I met in the café spoke about miracles and healings, but these were passing remarks in most cases, and I could not record our conversations. It would be good if someone in the future could gather all of these devotees experiences together as there are so many stories on everyone's lips. People tell of Sharavana's tremendous energy or how he sometimes does things that are hard to explain. For example, one middle-aged woman told me how Sharavana told her to gather together several different coloured Kumkuma powders with Tailam oil and place them on his head.

"I was amazed that it stayed there. On a normal person, it would have slid off immediately as it is so oily," she said. "Swami then continued to do poojas and was even dancing vigorously, but the pile of Kumkuma and Tailam didn't move at all. Every grain of Kumkuma remained perfectly in place, and the oil did not budge. He continued like this for more than two and a half hours. What I was seeing was impossible."

She also told me about her first-ever meeting with Sharavana. "Before encountering swami, I was a follower of Amma. I met her when I was twelve. I was told that I could ask her something, so I asked her if she could give me peace of mind. Amma just looked at me and gave a loving smile.

"Sharavana is younger than me, so he would have been about five years old at the time 40 years ago when I saw Amma. The opening words that Sharavana said to me when I first met him were, 'I believe you are looking for peace of mind?'

"His words touched my heart, and I have been a devotee ever since."

The devotees who surround Sharavana come from all walks of life. I met simple villages as well as multi-millionaires. Nagendra, nicknamed Naga, is a successful businessman from Malaysia. He had an intriguing story to share with me:

Naga: Swami stays in my house whenever he comes to Malaysia. He travelled for about 20 to 25 days in Malaysia and travelled from South to North, visiting many temples and sacred places. I gave him the use of my car, so I was fortunate to travel with him and together with other aspirants we were able to have many beautiful experiences.

Craig: Of these, which one most impressed you?

Naga: I have an office in my house, and on a table, in front of where I sit, I have a photo of swami. I was feeling despondent as I'd just had some bad business news. You know how it is all businesses have their ups and downs. That evening at about 10:30 pm, I looked at his photo and said to Swami, 'why am I going through so many problems, and why am I not happy? I am feeling so very stressed. After knowing you, I need your help!'

I kept on like this for some time. Blah, blah blah talking and complaining to his photograph for about 15 minutes. Then I was interrupted by the phone. It was Sharavana calling me! He said, 'Why do you keep complaining when I am right beside you. I am beside you, and still, you are worried!'

That really shocked me. I said, 'Swami, I have been speaking to your photo. Were you listening?' He replied, 'Yes, I am alive there. I have been listening to you.'

Even now, as I recount the story, I get goosebumps. This all happened when I was a new follower of swami. It made me realise that he is not a joke. If I talk to him in a photo, he can reply. From that day onwards, I have another level of understanding, and I invite him into my heart. I know now that I am not with a simple astrologer or something. No, I know that he is above all of that. This experience has brought me very close to him, and I know that I can trust him, and I want to help his mission. His mission is straightforward. It is to help the poor and to make poor people happier. They need help, so we must help. That is his most important work.

He also tells us that we must take care of our family, mother, father, brother and sister and make sure that everyone is okay. Don't forget them in life. If you forget them, you lose the biggest asset in your life. Until the last day, you must take care of them. These are the things that he has taught us. We must care for poor people and our families. This comes first.

Craig: Oh! Good to hear that from a business person!

Naga: I'll take care of my parents until their dying day. They stay at my house. This is a blessed opportunity.

Craig: Has he ever told you about your future?

Naga: I have known him for about ten years now, and he has told me many things about what's ahead. He has told me when to be careful or to watch out and tells me when business will be good or if a huge opportunity is ahead. I may spot a significant business opportunity and will ask him what I should do. Sometimes he tells me to think about it or to wait or not to act now. He may say, don't waste your time or tell me to grab the opportunity immediately. He is always right, and because of this, my business has been fruitful and successful. So I am happy that I have someone to guide me and give me certainty in important decisions.

Craig: Have you also had guidance in other areas of your life?

Naga: He has also advised about marriage. There was a man who wanted to marry my daughter and make a formal proposal. I asked swami about this. He said, 'no, this man is not suitable. I will bring a capable person for her. She is my daughter too. You don't have to worry.'

He knows everything. You really don't have to worry.

Craig: And is she now married?.

Naga: No, but once he says these words, I know it will all be all right.

There was another incident that you may find

interesting. A new Murugan temple was under construction near my house, so I took a look. I was invited into the temple for a small dinner. I began visiting the temple regularly, and within a month, the temple was complete.

I would go there to pray, and as I prayed, I thought about swami. On this occasion, I circled the temple's Arasa Maram tree (Also known as the Peepal tree) and bowed and chanted to the player and Ganpati. I then walked to my car and drove home.

Soon after I arrived, the phone rang. It was swami calling from London to make arrangements for his trip to Malaysia.

We talked for a while about the arrangements, and then he says, 'This morning, I saw you circling a tree. I was watching you. You were circling an Arasa Maram tree. You were chanting, and near you chose Ganpati.' He had told me exactly what had been happening earlier. I was shocked. Swami is a Miracleman!

Craig: He does appear to know what everyone is up to. Before he visited our house in England, he told my wife and me that our home is in a green leafy setting, has all cream walls, and we own a white cat.

Naga: I am a patron of his organization, and I plan his programmes in Malaysia. He may stay for up to 20 days and will meet up to 20,000 people in the temple hall over the period. And yet, he knows every one of them individually.

Craig: He knows absolutely everyone personally?

Naga: Yes, and he helps them all. On one occasion, a couple came to see him and were booked to consult with him. The wife had a growth in her stomach – a suspected cancer - and was due to have an operation. They came to swami hoping to get a blessing and maybe a cure. Swami gave them turmeric powder and told them to take it with a bit of water for three days and three nights.

They did as instructed, and on the fifth day after seeing swami, they went to the hospital for their medical check and to have the final X-Ray before setting the operation date. The doctors had taken a set of X-Rays three weeks before, and it was clear that the condition was getting progressively worse.

There was a long wait for three hours before the new X-Rays were presented to the couple. This was a private clinic, so usually, the diagnosis is quick. However, the doctors seemed to be in a fluster and were taking an extraordinarily long time.

'We have been discussing your X-Rays for two hours,' he said to the couple. 'What did you do in the last few days?' They showed her the old X-Ray and the new X-Ray and said, 'As you can see. The growth is missing!'

These accounts of miracles are just a few of the many circulating on the ashram grapevine. Unfortunately, I could only pin down a few people to interview and record their experiences, but if you would like to read more, a growing number are published on the ashram website at omsharavanabhavamatham.org. These include fascinating accounts about healing and reports from people who have sacred ash (vibhuti) manifesting on photographs of swami.

Raising the Vibration

The people I talked to about their experiences with

Sharavana Baba were lucky to have a direct and close relationship with swami. It was clear to me that in the future, it will not be as easy as it is now to have one to one conversations with Sharavana. Just as the guru Amma hugs every devotee, so too Sharavana will give every visitor a short insightful message about their spiritual life. In time, the crowds will be around him, and the opportunities for one to one contact will be few.

There were people here who had previously been followers of Sathya Sai Baba. Some devotees had previously been followers of contemporary gurus such as Mata Amritanandamayi (Amma), Swami Paramsanson Nithyananda and Dr Pillai. I had some fascinating discussions with these intelligent, thoughtful people who were visiting the ashram. One question that kept coming up in our conversations was why Sharavana resonated the energy of Sai Baba of Shirdi, also known as Shirdi Sai Baba, an Indian spiritual master who died in 1918. What was this energy, and how could we react with it to quicken our enlightenment?

Unlike Sathya Sai Baba, Sharavana does not claim to be the reincarnation of Sai Baba of Shirdi but says that a part of that avatar's energy is living within him. Just as the human body has muscle memory, our soul remembers our times from previous lives. When we chant mantras, this energy is enhanced and awakened. This is why an all-inclusive mantra such as the Subrahmanya Ashtothram that includes all the names of God is powerful. It will trigger positive God orientated vibrations that remain in us from your previous births.

Our bodies contain a bio-energy from our

previous lives that creates our physical body and its potential for health or illness. A more refined version of this energy manifests as our psychology, and a nuanced version constructs our astral body. These energies interact, but if we can attune ourselves with the highest vibrations of these 'God Particles', we become free of all ailments and disease. We inherit these 'God Particles' from our past lives. We must synchronise with the purest vibrations to not be trapped again in a cycle of wrong actions inherited from previous lives. Clearly, these devotees were not talking about the 'Higgs Boson God Particles'; they were describing in a clear way how the prana energy works with the koshas.

Sharavana, they said, has a unique ability to borrow from the god particles of previous gurus. This is why we see him manifest the qualities of Sai Baba of Shirdi and other great souls. When great beings attain the highest levels of enlightenment, their power becomes omnipresent and can manifest in souls capable of being a conduit of this energy. In some respects, it is like a highly refined form of trance mediumship in which the channel is connecting with the highest spiritual powers.

The experience of the enlightenment is the same for all beings, but its expression is different. It appears from what these devotees were saying that enlightened beings seem to have no sense of Jeeva – individual selfhood – but manifest collectively through any enlightened channel. Albert Einstein, for example, was, they said, a manifestation of the vibration of the famous Tamil Siddha called Bogar, who lived sometime between 550 and 300 BC. Of course, there's no proof of this, and Einstein never expressed this sentiment, but he was undoubtedly a man who knew how to use powerful, intuitive abilities. He said, "The intellect has little to do on the road to discovery. There comes a leap in consciousness, call it intuition or what you will, the solution comes to you, and you don't know how or why." And many of the things he has to say reflect many Indian ideas though today, there are also many false quotations by him floating around the internet.

I'm not sure I necessarily agree with all of these ideas, but it was certainly food for thought. It was undoubtedly true that when you go to an ashram, the vibrations lift the spirit. Rarely in daily life, we have time to engage in profound philosophical discussion, and rarer still do we have the time to contemplate and digest new ideas. We can grab moments for deep thought here and there at home, but there is time for serious and uninterrupted spiritual reflection on the ashram.

The idea that everything is vibration is not new. Within Spiritualism, we talk about how the people from the spirit world have to slow their vibration to communicate with a medium. Similarly, a medium has to raise their vibration to make contact with the spirit. When the two oscillations are in harmony, a spirit communication can occur. The medium's mind blends with the spirit communicator and relays information to prove the survival of human consciousness after death.

I have always believed that consciousness - before and after death - radiates from the quantum world. It is the seat of identity. The quantum world is the spirit. When we are on earth, the brain becomes the conduit through which the soul finds expression. Our brain is simply a receiver. When we die, we step back again into the pure realms of the spirit. Behind our material world and the next lies the absolute stillness of the great ocean of existence beyond all vibration. Spiritual practice and the guidance of a guru awakens us to the complete peace of our true Self.

It is interesting to take these ideas a little further by thinking about how the great gurus can influence and change our vibration level. Some of the people I met explained how they would invite the guru's energy to change them on every level of their being. As we saw, Sharavana's energy can cause many physical changes to a person and even bring them back from the brink of cancer. The guru's energy first touches the person's spirit body and, through it, changes the physical body. By attuning ourselves to the resonance of the guru, our vibrations synchronise, and we can draw upon the ineffable energy of the divine.

I recalled how Sharavana had once told Jane and me that we had been with him at the time of Sai Baba of Shirdi. We three indeed seemed to resonate together when we met. It was like meeting an old friend. And, of course, Jane and I felt incredibly uplifted and empowered by every encounter with Sharavana. My own experience tells me that people like Sharavana have the power to subtly change our vibrations and leave us feeling high and joyful. Who knows on how many levels he works with us?

The divine consciousness I spoke about is beyond quality. It, therefore, transcends happiness or any attribution we can use to describe it. We may call it bliss, love, peace, the divinity of God, but nothing can express what is beyond mind and form. We may feel a sense of happiness when we are around spiritually enlightened people because it reminds us of who we really are. As we approach this 'state' embodied by the enlightened soul, we have feelings of love, joy, bliss and indescribable happiness as we come close to our reality.

There are many new-age gurus out there who offer quick fixes for happiness, but most of these thrive on peddling misconceptions and easy answers. The basic premise is that if we can visualize what we want and add emotional power to that wish, we will attract abundance. A whole industry has arisen to help us 'manifest abundance', 'think and grow rich', 'script the law of attraction', and so on. By using what they claim are secrets from the ancients and scientific methods, you can effortlessly attract everything you want – love, name, fame, money, happiness and so on. They claim that similar things attract each other, so positive thoughts bring positive results, and negative thoughts bring negative results. All we have to do is think about what we want, and we will get it.

The happiness being sold by these - mainly American - teachers is material happiness. But as necessary as these things are, they are nonetheless temporary. The pain of loss of these gains is greater than having them in the first place – something the psychologists call 'negative bias'. We are hard-wired to feel the sting of a rebuke more powerfully than we feel the joy of praise, recall insults better than congratulation, and remember traumatic experiences better than positive ones. Loss creates more pain than the joy of gain. This tendency evolved to protect us from danger. The archaic man had to be alert to dangerous threats in his environment. Whoever paid attention to bad things were more likely to survive.

All the positive thinking in the world cannot alter the fact that all is in a state of change. As soon as we decide permanent happiness is found in material things, our friends ageing, disease and death drop in to remind of us our foolishness.

From a physics standpoint, it's opposites that attract, not similars but also the arguments don't, in my opinion, correspond with ancient teachings either. What's missing is the law of karma. If I were a perfect pure being and free of all karma, then I probably could attract anything I desire – except, of course, I would have transcended desire and would have no need to attract the shallow things promised by the happiness gurus. The reality is that I have brought the effects of my past life karma into this life that will unfold as need be; I am also generating karma with my thoughts and actions now that will determine my future. Karma determines what the universe will give me.

If I want to manifest abundance, I have to do the spiritual work. If we think good thoughts and do good actions, then we pave the way for good things ahead. Unpleasant situations result from lingering karma, which we can alter and resolve with suitable activities. Yoga, kriya techniques, spiritual worship, devotional acts, holy pilgrimages, chanting mantra, meditation, charitable acts, building temples, planting trees, and so on are all remedies to negate negative karma. If we want to manifest abundance, we have to do the work. It is no good sitting around and greedily visualizing what you think you should get. As Sai Baba explained, it is better to give and forgive than get and forget. Through generosity, you will get back exactly what you need for happiness that is not dependent on transient material things. And most importantly, without underlying contentment, there can be no lasting happiness.

The bedrock of reality is non-material, and it is the place where our consciousness is seated or at least it should be. If we desert our throne and seek contentment in the objective world, we are soon lost, and our power is gone. We do not have to renounce the world, but we need to be seated in the right place. Sharavana often reminds us – as I have already explained – to live from the inside. Once we are centred within – and in a state of acceptance - we find that our thoughts will have a powerful effect upon events and the world around us. Thoughts are things and fly from us to do our bidding in the world. They have a minimal impact when powered by selfishness and greed but gain tremendous power if fueled by love.

Every thought, both now and in the past, affects what is happening to us. Generating good thoughts today will clear our path for the future, but we appear to have no control over the thoughts we had in the past and our many past lives. These, and the thoughts of other people who responded to our actions, create a shoal of troubles that follow us from life to life. The memory of the actions and thoughts have gone, but their residual vibrations remain. This is karma. Some of this karmic energy has been released already and shapes our present life. Some are yet to be released. We are generating karma now, and the good and bad results of these energies will shape our lives in the future.

We are creating karma all the time and sometimes creating negative karma without realizing it, and sometimes another person's negative karma can rub off on us. If we step into someone's karmic bubble, we may feel the sting of their dark emotions and energy. However, if you are working from a high spiritual level of love and compassion, you will not be affected. Negative karma is generated when we are down, but it can also occur while we are happy. An interesting message from the Jiva Naadi from Agastya said, "Mistakes committed when someone is in a normal state or even feeling sad is nothing compared to the mistakes done when someone is extremely happy. Therefore, it is important to have a balanced state of mind, also known as non-attachment. This truth is taught in the 62nd and 63rd chapters of Sundara Kandam." (This naadi teaches that we can clear negative karma if we read the 5th book of the Ramayana called the Sundara Kandam.)

Our hopes for happiness look pretty bleak if we have masses of accumulated karma to either support or thwart our efforts. Fortunately, Karma is not an iron law: we can modify it. One remedy is grace. Divine grace permeates all things and blows like a gentle wind around us. If we open ourselves to it, we can sail easily over the ocean of karma. We may be fortunate enough to have just enough good karma to lead us to meet the right people, read the right book or meet the right guru who can open your mind to spiritual knowledge. The grace domiciled in a guru can quench the fires of desire, anger and greed that befoul the heart. This grace can bring Ananda – a bliss that is the highest form of happiness that comes when we connect to the divine. A sincere seeker – through devotion – can draw down the grace of God that will be like a pain-killer that soothes you as the innocuous karma unfolds.

Another remedy is what Krishna in the Bhagavadgita calls Karma Yoga. He explains to his pupil Ajuna about the discipline of action and that renouncing the world is a false path. "A man does not attain freedom from the results of action by abstaining from actions and does not approach perfection simply by renunciation," says Krishna. He explains that the fruits of action are to be renounced, not the action itself. Unlike the greedy teachings of the American 'Happiness Gurus,' I mentioned earlier, the way to bliss is not through desiring rewards or triumphing in the egotism that accompanies accomplishment but through selfless action. We simply do what we do without expectation of reward, knowing that everything is God and everywhere God unfolding. The truth is that nothing can be ours. We own nothing, and yet we simultaneously own everything, for we too are God.

Avoid gurus and religions that offer you quick fixes for happiness. These epiphanies do not last long, but every good thought and deed you do will echo in the universal mind for eternity.

Having developed much of my spiritual power through Spiritualism, I still hold with the fifth principle that forms the basis of SNU Spiritualism. It was channelled by the trance medium Emma Hardinge Britten and simply says 'Personal Responsibility. "This Principle is the one which places responsibility for wrongful thoughts and deeds where it belongs, with the individual," says SNU Spiritualism. "It is not possible for any other person or outside influence to interfere with our spiritual development unless we are willing to allow this. As we are given freedom of choice (free will), so also are we given the ability to recognise what is right and wrong for our own spirituality. We are personally responsible for all our words, deeds and thoughts."

Although I disagree with most of the other principles of Spiritualism, this one has always stuck with me. For this reason, I am not a devotee of any guru, whether it be Sathya Sai Baba, Sharavana Baba, Agastya speaking to me through the Naadis, my spirit guides or any of the wonderful holy men and women I have met on my journey. All can lift our hearts to the highest high, but in the end, only I can awaken in enlightenment. No one else can do it for me.

If we look too much for guidance from without, we may forget to look within. It is easy to forget to rely on the God who dwells in our hearts. Enlightened saints, Siddhas and holy people inspire me, but eventually, we must have the courage to be our own masters. A tree does not grow in the shadow of another tree. It must stand alone in the sunlight.

Shed Material Thoughts

A good deal of what happens on the ashram is about clearing karma. One method is to participate in a Homa (also known as Havan or a Yajna). The Homa is a fire ritual performed on special occasions by a group of Hindu priests. A massive eight foot high Homa was under construction for the main Maha Shivratri ceremony. Smaller homas were available in the temple areas for fire rituals before the main event, and I could sponsor one of these for my requirements. On the way to my sponsored event, I was able to get a quick interview with Sharavana

Baba. I decided to ask him about mediumship and bereavement.

"Swami, one of the most significant causes of unhappiness in people's lives comes when they lose someone to death. In my work as a medium, I try to connect the two worlds. Can you give me some guidance about this?"

"All things are connected," he said after a few moments of silence. "People must shed the material thoughts; then divine thoughts will come. When we shed the material thoughts and have divine thoughts, then the worlds connect."

"So mediumship works if we have divine thoughts? It works by love.

"Yes, yes," he replies as he pats me on the back. "Good answer."

I agree with Sharavana that divine thoughts are needed when a medium links to the next world. I have met many mediums and psychics who work far from this ideal and sometimes still appear to get correct information from the spirit world. My first mediumship teacher Peter Close told me that the spirit will always try to communicate through any channel they can find. However, it's like using a broken violin that sounds bad when even a maestro uses it. Give the musician a good instrument, and glorious music can come forth.

Innermost sincerity is the trigger for divine thoughts. How can we ever know the divine truth if we lie, for we also lie to ourselves? Many mediums (and gurus) profess all sorts of extravagant claims and will cheat to qualify their assertions. But to know the truth, we must have the purest or pure hearts. Only the person who possesses complete sincerity and trustworthiness can develop authentic spirituality. Without total honesty with ourselves and the world, we can never directly know the universal truth. It takes courage to strip away the preconceptions and egotism that eclipse the light of inner truth. And only when we know our nature can we perceive the nature of others and thereby help them understand their life's purpose. If we can help others develop their true nature, we invoke the transformative powers of the divine. We become the channel of a heavenly force that can nourish all who come in contact with us. This state is what it is to be a genuine psychic, medium or guru. The bedrock of success is innermost sincerity.

In these troubled times, it is hard shedding material thoughts, as Sharavana suggests. Most people strive for gratification in some form or other, but the pandemic has helped them escape this trap for some. Many of the usual paths to material happiness are blocked during the pandemic, making many people rethink their needs. Lockdowns and restrictions make it impossible to find the dubious highs that people think of as happiness. We cannot travel, go to pubs, bars and parties. Socialising with large groups of friends is stopped and the cinemas, theatre and music festivals are closed. Being forced to slow down and stop initially creates frustration, tension, and social unrest, but I hope that some people will set new goals with a newfound spirit of acceptance. We may now strive for tranquillity rather than satisfy endless cravings, and, as Sharavana says, spiritual thoughts will come.

The philosophers of ancient Greece recognized that a robust inner equilibrium is born when a person lets go of material cravings. They called this Ataraxia. It is described as a clear internal state of stable equanimity that is free from distress and worry. Pyrrhonist philosophers said ataraxia is essential for bringing about eudaimonia (happiness) for a person. For them and the Stoic and Epicurean philosophers to follow, it represented life's ultimate purpose. Although the schools of Greek philosophy put different emphasis on Ataraxia, all consider it central to understanding the soul. As I understand it, Ataraxia is the untroubled and tranquil condition that comes when we are free of attachments and accept things as they are - neither denying nor affirming anything.

Ataraxia is a state that is free from distress and worry. This mindset is experienced and cultivated internally. Instead of chasing material thoughts, ataraxia suggests striving for a feeling of tranquillity. It is a resting state of peace from which happiness naturally emerges and rubs off on everyone around you. The philosophy encourages us to relax, have fun and make the best of every day. This method will make you flourish.

It seems that the ancient Greeks were there centuries ago. They'd got it together, but now we have to relearn these things. Perhaps modern man has misunderstood happiness? Today we seek happiness by doing things like shopping, having sex, getting things, entertainment, etc. We are obedient to all that consumer society throws at us. We get conned by false ideas such as being in love is the only happiness, but then feel let down when people do not live up to our expectations.

For many, the idea of romantic love can be an

obstacle to happiness as we have too high expectations. The initial excitement of passionate love is often mistaken as the goal of life and is the ultimate happiness. Many of the people who come to see Jane or me for psychic readings are hoping to be shown a way to find their soulmate. But this soulmate idea is fraught with dangers. The hope is that once they find this elusive soulmate, all will be perfect; they will find their heart's desire and live happily ever after.

Unfortunately, many couples discover that the infatuation of love fades quickly, and soon they see their soulmate in a completely different light. The euphoria of passion is impossible to sustain. We are not built to be forever high on the love drug. It's a lie; it's a con spun by Cupid, a sneaky god who takes pleasure in bringing inappropriate people together. If we marry in haste, as Oscar Wilde said, we will repent at leisure.

Lasting happy relationships come not from endless burning passion but from what the psychologists call companionate love. Companionate love is a love that is sustainable, slow to develop and brings loyalty, affection, intimacy, and commitment. For relationships to be happy, you need an underlying companionate love with the occasional bursts of passionate love. And if you really want a relationship to thrive, you need a shared spirituality and a preparedness to make sacrifices for one another. You are not expecting someone to make you happy but are helping one another up the ladders of life. With all this – and a little humour too – your relationships will be happy.

Similar criteria apply to your relationship with a guru. Some people dive in with an inappropriate passion. They expect the guru to solve all of their problems instantly then become disillusioned when it does not happen. They may even become spiritually disturbed and turn against the guru. No one is going to wave a magic wand and make all your problems disappear. There's work to do. It is better to have a sustained relationship with the guru. Let the guru become your lifelong friend.

The Hellenistic idea was that happiness comes with the absence of inner disturbance, and we are naturally happy when we cease to crave. The philosophy encourages us to see our problems – even things like the pandemic and other seemingly huge issues - as just tiny specs in the big picture. The Roman Emperor Marcus Aurelius, another Stoic philosopher, summed it up when he wrote, "Dwell on the beauty of life. Watch the stars, and see yourself running with them."

Homa for Health and Wellbeing

When I'm in India, I have the feeling that I'm in contact with the last remnants of the classical world. Like the Sumerians, Egyptians, Greeks and Romans, India remains polytheistic and retains many rituals and magical ceremonies that must have been common in distant history. With the chants, smoke, incense and giant fires of the Homa, I can easily imagine that I'm in ancient times and perhaps a part of the Isis, Eleusinian or Mithraic Mysteries from long ago. India is a place that continues to connect us with the riddles of the collective unconscious.

After talking with Sharavana, I made my way to the Homa fire ceremony that I had sponsored. I had done some of these ceremonies before when I did the karma clearing remedies from my naadi leaves. The energy they create is intense both on a physical level with the rising flames and on an energetic level. Modern man has rejected all of this in favour of science. To the rationalist, the idea of healing with a ritualized fire is superstition and hogwash, but from my own experience, I knew that there is far more to this than meets the eye. For example, one of my naadi readings revealed that my mother would die soon as she had cancer on her lung. A few weeks later, an X-ray revealed that she had a dangerous shadow on her lung. The naadi instructed me to have a special Homa performed by four priests and that this would clear the condition. I said nothing to my mother but did as instructed. Her following scan revealed that the shadow had disappeared entirely. She knew nothing of what I had done until I told her later, so it could not be self-healing due to the placebo effect. The Homa had remotely effected a cure without her knowing anything about it.

The Homa today was to bring healing to the family. I also included in the list of names my friend in India, Mr Prakash. You may know from my other books that he was one of the naadi readers I had travelled with to do my remedies. We had since become good friends.

Unfortunately, Mr Prakash had become dangerously ill just before I set out for India. He required urgent and immediate heart surgery but could not afford the costs. I hastily helped set up a 'go fund me' website, announced it on my YouTube channel and told my patrons of the Hamilton Parker Foundation about it. Within a few days, we were able to raise enough money for the operation. Coincidentally this Homa was to take place at the exact moment he was being taken into surgery.

Since the earliest times, the element of fire was associated with the gods. It seems like a living being as fire appears to eat its fuel, grows, transforms, and dies. Wherever you look, fire is a symbol of divinity. The Ancient Zoroastrians believe the fire to have been "the most holy spirit" in the Old Testament God gave Moses a sign through a burning bush and Greek legends tell of how Prometheus stole the fire from the gods. These Vedic Homa rituals form an unbroken line back to these ancient times.

I was given a seat near the Homa fires as the priests chanted Vedic mantras and threw fruit, herbs and seeds into the hearth. The other sponsors and I received a tray of plant offerings that we put into the fire as we say the words 'S-w-ah-h-ah'. (Svāhā means 'well said' or 'so be it' and is chanted to offer an oblation to the gods at the end of a mantra.) Sharavana then joins us, and the rituals continue to become part of the public event. A queue forms, and everyone present can now add their offerings to the fire.

I thought about my family, friends, and Mr Prakash, who was now having his heart operation. My thoughts turned to the dead through the commotion of echoing chants clashing bells, and the pungent smells of burning fruits, ghee and incense. At that moment, I had a potent feeling of my grandfather's spirit standing beside me. I had felt something similar before in India when I climbed the sacred mount Arunachala. My grandfather had mapped unexplored areas of Africa in his early life and had brushed with unfamiliar cultures, traditions and rituals. I could sense that he was delighted with what I was doing.

At the end of the Homa, Sharavana gave a public address in the main hall. He spoke in Malayalam about the importance of worshipping the ancestors. The translation was hard to follow. I noticed how the number of people cramming the hall had grown since yesterday. Many more villagers had arrived, but also I saw more western faces in the crowd. There will be huge crowds surrounding Sharavana Baba one day, and it will be hard to have the interviews and intimate connection we enjoy today. It is nice to think that I played a small part in helping his message reach the multitude through my books and YouTube channel.

"I would like us today to extend our thoughts to our ancestors," said the translator as Sharavana spoke. I could see that Sharavana spoke with elegance and fluidity, but the translator narrated the discourse with disjointed sentences in an impossible to understand accent. He spoke like an Indian version of Stanley Unwin, but I suppose he was doing his best, though much was lost.

Sharavana spoke about the importance of mind, intellect, wisdom and how family, wealth and work were blessings. We have all these things, but none of it would exist if it were not for the struggles of our ancestors. For millions of years, that had helped humankind get to this point. We should therefore be grateful to our ancestors.

"Family life is rightly important to everyone," said Sharavana. "Working life is meaningful too. With no job, we have no respect. With no money, we gain no respect. But if we have these things, do they bring happiness? We must find real happiness. Money does not matter: it is a big illusion. Money can take away our time. Happiness is more important. Happiness is a blessing: it brought you here.

Sharavana goes on to talk about today's homas and the astrological importance of this moment in time. He speaks about the nine planets and the 27 birth stars and how they hold special significance now. Some chanting and events followed his address, and events concluded with the audience each lighting a small ghee lamp.

I was able to pick up on the theme of happiness again after the talk when I had a few moments with him at darshan. He knew, of course, that I was writing the book, and happiness would be its theme, so I picked up from my last chat with him.

"Swami," I said, "one of the things that I think causes much unhappiness in people is the fear of the future. In this uncertain world with so many international troubles, what advice can you give people about facing the future?"

"The main problem is that people plan too much," he replied. The divine plan is already there. You need have no fear."

"So we should just trust the future?"

"Yes, yes. Just be happy."

CHAPTER 21

Ancient Oracles

With the waning yellow moon high in the early evening sky and the hot temperature of the day settling into an uncomfortable sultriness, a strange group of odd-looking men entered the ashram. There was an immediate commotion, noise and frantic activity at their unexpected arrival. These men, I discovered later, are the Velichappadu – a mysterious sect of sadhus from Valluvanad. They look terrifying but are revered in Kerala. It was a highly auspicious sign for them to arrive so close to Maha Shivaratri.

The Velichappadu had wild unkempt hair that hung long down their backs and over their faces. Their bodies were smeared with turmeric and a white Bhasmam ash that is sacred to Shiva. Some carried round shields and wore tin armour over their bright red clothes. Around their necks were heavy ritual ornaments and garlands, and about the waist, they wore wide belts studded with small curling bronze bells.

The one that approached me had the wild red eyes of a Samurai warrior. He put out his tongue till it touched his chin and pointed at me with his sword that had a curved end like a sickle. He stepped forward as if ready to behead me with it then, to my surprise, gently placed the blade onto the top of my head.

A man stood to my side patted me on the back. "Sir, this is a very great blessing, sir," he said with a beamish smile across his face. "Very good, very good."

And there's me thinking I've just been knighted.

I found out later that the Velichappadu are followers of Kali and can become possessed by the Goddess Bhadrakaali, one of the fierce forms of the Great Goddess Shakti.

The Velichappadu live in a few temples across Kerala, where they do Pooja, meditation and penance. They will chant and pray to Bhadrakaali until they enter a trance and then begin a slow rhythmic Thullal dance until the goddess possesses them. Sometimes during their ecstatic trance, they cut their forehead with their sword to signify their unshakable devotion.

With blood-red faces, the Thullal dance comes to a frantic conclusion, and the deity speaks. She talks through the mouthpiece of the Velichappadu and makes predictions. Like the ancient oracles of Delphi, their language is strange, frenzied and hard to decipher. They often make prophecies and give solutions to problems asked about by the devotees. Often these require translation and interpretation by their assistants.

The Velichappadu are known as the 'revealers of

light'. They are oracles who tell the future and are the mediators between the deity and its devotees.

Kali Bhava Samadhi

Soon after this, Sharavana dropped into a trance called a Bhava samadhi, when a god or higher spirit enters the body to dance or speak through them. Sharavana's helpers guide him into a chair, and the crowd press around him to hear what is said. They tell me that swami is channelling the goddess Kali.

Sharavana wails like a strange animal and then cries and whimpers like a small child in distress. The trance is reminiscent of what we saw in London when he channelled the Naga. Soon he is entirely overshadowed by the goddess. His mother walks forward and raises her hands towards him. His face distorts into odd-looking shapes and looks as he writhes around on his chair. He speaks in a loud babbling voice, then reaches out suddenly and grabs a large camphor flame to his side and puts it out with his hands. He drops into a somnambulistic sleep and reaches out again, this time putting his hands into a large silver tray of turmeric and vibhuti nearby.

Next, he speaks in a slow, sleepy whisper and the crowd strain to hear what is said. Two scribes beside him listen intently and write down everything he has to say. These are the prophecies for the future given by the goddess Kali.

After a period of silence, while still sitting in the chair, swami stands, and we follow him in silence along the dusty path to the naga temple and pit. Partway, he stops, stares at a solitary star in the sky, and says, "The nine planets' energy is in the one-star".

We move on, snaking our way around the naga temple area and then descending the steps into the giant pit beside the temple. Swami's trance deepens again, and he slowly begins to dance like a woman, whirling around swinging on a pole and waving his saffron shawl. When the dance ends, he begins speaking again in Malayalam. A man stood nearby translates as best he could:

"Swami is saying that he is working on a level that we cannot understand. There is no need to think much. Just follow the truth that you have intuitively understood here today. Follow that truth and let it uplift you. It will lead you to a path that you did not expect.

"We take different forms to fulfil nature. If we want to do some Kriyas for the betterment of humanity, we can use our bodies. You have divine energies coming through your body now. If you can understand this, then you are truly here today. You are fulfilling your sacred duties. You have done much already. Try to obey the truth within you, and this day will be very good for you. We can acquire different forms at any time. That is why I show this to devotees who can understand.

"Understand that Babaji is just Maya. We do not have a name or form. What is there in the form? How long can anything exist? This world is not eternal. The one who is above all this is it. To fulfil the mission that we have come for in this birth, we acquire another form. Many souls are in Babaji. When we are thirsty, we take the water from the well. Babaji is the rope that lets you draw the water from the well. We pray and bless your work.

"A virus is upon the world. It is the first. There are

two more to come. What can we do to stop the virus? What can you do? First, we must pray. It comes, but it will be neutralized. Whichever country it comes to, think of it as my country. One day it may be my country, it hits. Tomorrow it may be yours. Let it teach us to see the world as one. The world is mount Kailash. It is all the dreams of Vishnu. Vishnu placed you in the warm womb of the world. Brahma made your life essence, Vishnu sustains you, and Shiva brings you to the world."

Most of the days leading up to Maha Shiavathi are not as dramatic as this. My time is spent watching Sharavana perform poojas and give talks, talking to people about spirituality or listening to the mantras chanted throughout the day. It is a friendly place and fine for anyone travelling entirely on their own.

The mantras can be profoundly engaging if you can find a spot to sit back and absorb them. Some of the Brahmins doing the chanting had travelled the long journey from Bombay. There were 300 or so verses sung – none of which I understood – but the vibrations of the Sanskrit are enough to lift the soul. You don't need to understand them to get the benefit, and I found them to be magically restorative.

Earlier, Sharavana had spoken to me to say that he knew that I was exhausted, and this is why he had placed his hands on me and given me a bolt of energy. I was sitting in the crowd when he walked up to me, put his hands on my shoulders and flooded a massive wave of energy through me. I have sat with some of the best spiritual healers in the past, but the bolt of energy swami gave me at that moment was beyond compare.

The mantras and the ambience of the place were now further helping me to feel energized again. Trips to India are always very tiring, but this one had somehow washed me out, although far less physically challenging than my previous journeys. I think I had been tired before leaving, and together with the hard flights, jet lag and late nights, it had all caught up with me. But now things were fine, and I could enjoy the experience. As I watched the life unfolding in the ashram witnessed the devotion of many of the people here. There were none of the over-the-top devotional indulgences that you see around some gurus. People here were much more sensible, but I was not like them in many ways.

The next time I met Sharavana, he spoke to me about the healing jolt and said he realized how tired I was. I thanked him for his powerful restoration but felt that I should not be treated differently to other visitors to the ashram. I said that I consider him a close friend and have massive respect for his knowledge, but it is not in my nature to be a devotee. It didn't seem to bother him at all. He was all smiles as he said, "Friendship first. Then worship. Relationship strong."

As I've already said elsewhere, for me becoming a devotee of a guru or avatar is not my way. I have been weaned through Spiritualism to embrace the idea that we have free will and must take responsibility for our actions. Although the philosophy of spiritualism is generally a little shallow, this principle of 'personal responsibility' is one of my personal spiritual values pillars. That's not to say that taking a devotional path is a bad thing. The narrow way to salvation is the quickest way for many people, but it is not one I feel I can take. Hard as it is, I have to forge my own path. Why should I need a guru? Surely the only place we will find what we are looking for is inside ourselves?

My next meeting with swami came after I sat in on the tail end of his talk. "We must live our life so that we are remembered after death," he said. "Be remembered for your honesty and sincerity. Honesty and sincerity bring everything into our lives. People also forget that prayer is more important than darshan. Prayer is internal. Prayer lights up something in the body." He explained that today's fire Homa would be performed to remove obstacles from our lives and negate karma's adverse effects.

After the event, I was able to join the darshan queue to have a quick meeting with Sharavana. Picking up on my previous comments about the need to follow a guru, I was thinking about how sometimes he answers the questions I have before I ask them. Could there be limits to what a guru can do for people? He looked at me with a wry look as if knowing what I was about to ask. "No questions today, swami," I said. "God is everywhere, so why should I ask questions?"

He bursts into laughter and points at himself. "Form limited. Other form unlimited!" We both giggle, and I make my way. Perhaps everything is possible?

Later that day, Sharavana talked about the omnipresence of a guru and spoke about how sometimes he will appear in people's dreams. I also received a reassuring text from Gopi, the brother of

Mr Parakash, who I had dedicated the Homa a few days ago. 'His operation was successful' read the text 'and he will be OK after four days.'

In India – and particularly around its ashrams – all sorts of miraculous stories circulate. One that was doing the rounds had recently been on WhatsApp about a 300-year-old man who had just been awakened from samadhi. The report said that this was a yogi in a transcendent, meditative state found alive after digging around a temple. He had been found in a 'haggard state covered with mud, blood and several sores oozing with fluid.' It turns out to be a false story of a falsely captioned medical picture of someone in Kazakhstan suffering from an aggravated case of psoriasis.

The story shows how susceptible people are to believe what they want to believe. We want things like this to be true, but just because you believe something is true does not necessarily mean it is true. We have to be discerning and do a little research too. However, when it comes to the stories about swami, I am placed in a unique position at the ashram because I could ask people about their first-hand experiences, and I was far more likely to get to the truth of the matter.

I thought about all of this as I tried to tackle some of the stories about swami and his healing powers. Then swami makes another synchronistic discourse, and again he seemed to be reading my thoughts.

"Belief is God," he said, "do not lose your belief."

Strangely enough, I'd just been having a fascinating

discussion with Ash about the power of belief and whether it could be a real force. Could it be that if we project our beliefs, they may act as a real force – something like the way the power of projected thought (psychokinesis) makes objects move? Could it be that the gods of India are real because they are the collective power of our projected thoughts? Our belief in them sustains them.

I am not entirely sure what Sharavana meant by his statement but often, what he has to say, has many layers of meaning. Who knows? Perhaps the ancient gods of Greece and Rome were once real and would still survive if only we continued to empower them with the energy of our belief. They may even have been seeded from the more ancient Indian gods that it has been argued saw their origin centuries before the last Ice Age. What powers have we instilled in these Tulpas? I am certainly of the opinion that thoughts are things and fly from us to influence the world. Could it be that the gods, on the one hand, represent aspects of the One God but are also the product of our mental energies entwined within our projected beliefs?

Swami said nothing about this the next time I met him but was clearly pleased that I was energetically making notes to write this book.

"Today, swami is very pleased you are writing a BIG book!" he joked. "You will spread swami's word."

"Snag is it's tough to report what you say accurately," I reply. Some of your translators speak with such a heavy accent that I cannot understand what they are saying. (I was thinking how they remind me of a stoned Stanley Unwin) "I'll have to look at your talks on YouTube for ideas."

"Do not worry about my words," he replies. "You are here so that you can understand Babaji."

With that, I was able to drop the idea of trying to transcribe his discourses. Throughout my stay, he had many beautiful things to say but hard to report. I suggest if you would like to know more, you look him up on YouTube.

Talking to some of the devotees about their experiences with Sharavana was also problematic. People were always on the move from one event to another, so I was only able to get a snapshot of stories most of the time. I'm sure that what people told me is just the tip of an enormous iceberg of miraculous stories.

On the day before Maha Shivaratri, I sit looking at my notebook and wondering how I could possibly write a book from all the small snippets I'd been given. I closed my eyes and went into a peaceful meditation. Perhaps I could get some guidance. Sharavana walked past me as I meditated, and I overheard him talking to someone else. I heard him say, "Tell only of what you have seen with your own eyes. The guru is always there. He will guide you." Was this a coincidence? Synchronicity? Or does Sharavana have a way of always saying exactly the right thing at the right time, even when his words are caught by people nearby? It is clear to me now that Sharavana is no ordinary man – his words and actions happen on many levels and have far-reaching effects.

When I open my eyes, I see someone sitting next to me and realise that it is one of the devotees I have gotten to know. "I waited until you finished your meditation," he said. "I felt that I must come over to you and show you this photograph that my friend has just sent me,"

He passed me his phone and showed me a photo of Sharavana covered in holy vibhuti ash. "This was just sent to me by an old school friend a few moments ago. He says that vibhuti ash is forming on all the photos he has of Sharavana Baba."

I was reminded of how vibhuti used to appear on the picture of Sathya Sai Baba and commented about this. Could Sharavana be on a similar level to Satya Sai Baba? "Sathya Sai is God. Sharavana is guru," he replied.

Later that day, several people spontaneously approached me with stories to tell. A woman from Canada also showed me a photo of Sharavana Baba with vibhuti materializing on it.

"A friend of the family was recently diagnosed with cancer, and it worried young daughter when she heard about it as it must have reminded her of when her grandparents died. She asked me, 'Where are Grandma and Grandpa?' and I would reply that they are with Shridi Sai – my way of meaning that they are dead."

"But she would have none of it", continued the Canadian Lady. "She went to our statue of Shridi Sai and prayed, 'Please return my grandparents, you've had them for long enough now.' She returned from the prayer room and told me that he will return them to the house tomorrow."

"The next day, vibhuti started to materialize on the statue of Shirdi Sai and also on pictures of Sharavana Baba. Within a day, there was loads of vibhuti pouring from the pictures of Sharavana Baba, and it is still happening. It pours from his eyes of the photograph."

"My daughter's miracle happened just four days ago, so we came here to the ashram to ask Swami about it. About a year ago, we brought our daughter to the ashram, and Sharavana said that she is a divine child and we must never scold her."

I decided to head back to my room and get some sleep in the late afternoon before the night-long vigil of Maha Shivaratri.

Maha Shivaratri

We are at the ashram, of course, to celebrate Maha Shivaratri. This is a Hindu festival that is celebrated every year in honour of Lord Shiva. It is also the night when Shiva performs the cosmic dance as Nataraja. This cosmic dance symbolises the interplay of dynamic and static divine energy flow. Within it are the five principles of cosmic energy: creation, preservation, destruction, illusion, and emancipation.

Every lunar month, there is a Shivaratri, but the Great (Maha) Shivaratri happens on the 13th night (waning Moon) and the 14th day of the Hindu month of Phalguna. This falls in either February or March. Ahead of the night of Maha Shivaratri, there are ten days of festivities and rituals that will gradually build in intensity. These festivities are a remembrance of 'overcoming darkness and ignorance in life and the world. It is like the guru who brings us from darkness into light.

I have always been intrigued by the strange figure

of Shiva. This blue-skinned and quirky character sits in serenity and yet is surrounded by snakes, spiders, and peculiar Ganadevata attendants? Shiva is a somewhat surreal and ambiguous figure. He is the Destroyer. He is the unfathomable emptiness into which creation must fall, and yet simultaneously, he is the Mahadeva, the highest of divine beings and creator of all that is. Dancing with Shakti - whose energy animates the Universe – together, they become a single reality of creation and destruction.

In his human form, Shiva is naked. His nudity shows his non-attachment to the material world. Shiva's body is ambiguous as it has male and female characteristics: no beard, a slightly feminine face, and a body with softly rounded contours. He is transcendent of opposites and division. Some sects of Hinduism believe that Shiva is the Supreme Lord of reality.

Shiva sits in meditation. The river Ganges flows from his long, uncombed hair. The new Moon is on his forehead; he has a cobra around his neck, a trident, and the white bull Nandi at his side. Around his neck, he wears a garland of 108 beads symbolising the elements of creation and in his hand is a rosary of 50 beads showing the 50 letters of the Sanskrit alphabet. In his ears are set two large rings showing that he has transcendent perceptions. His throat is stained blue, protecting us from the venom of impurity caused by stirring the spiritual powers in yoga practice. He sits on a tiger skin that points to power and mastery over the animal world. Shiva is associated with the Moon and also with fertility in the form of the Lingam.

Shiva has the third eye marked in the middle of his

forehead. This is the inner eye, the awakening, and perhaps the main hope for those participating in the Maha Shivaratri that it may bring us closer to self-realisation. The third eye chakra at the centre of the forehead is associated with the pineal gland. This chakra is also known as Ajna and is symbolized by two lotus leaves as it unites the brain's two hemispheres. The pineal gland has light-sensitive cells to receive and convey information about the current light-dark cycle from the environment. It is part of the endocrine system that secrete hormones into the bloodstream. From its unique position between the brain's two hemispheres, the pineal gland secretes melatonin, a derivative of serotonin, which generally contributes to feelings of well-being and happiness.

Perhaps the pineal gland is the actual seat of our happiness? Dr Rick Strassman, who conducted extensive research on near-death experiences in the 1990s, says that the pineal gland secretes the naturally occurring psychedelic hormone dimethyltryptamine (DMT). This hormone might trigger altered states of consciousness behind hypnagogic dreaming, near-death experiences and religious visions.

In Indian spiritual traditions, the third eye is the entryway into the ultimate forms of divine consciousness. In meditation, we can open this door and become aware of the foundation of our being as an infinite ocean of consciousness and bliss. Similar teachings are found in Taoism, Buddhism, Spiritualism, Theosophy and arguably also in Christianity. ('If therefore thine eye be single, thy whole body shall be full of light.' - Matthew 6:22) When this eye opens, a new dimension of reality reveals itself to the practitioner of meditation. It is a happiness beyond compare.

As we await the night of Maha Shivaratri and watch the moon move towards its final waning phase, I am struck by the idea that perhaps the ancients knew something about time that we may have lost. In this materialistic, externalized Age of Kali Yuga, time is reduced to a simple measurement. However, could time also be spiritual and did the ancients understand this when they made the first calendars? I was told that the Hindu calendar or Panchang system gives each year a specific name and a spiritual meaning. The year 2019 was a 'Vikari year', meaning 'repulsive year'. My time here in India is at the start of 2020 is a 'Sharvari year' meaning darkness which certainly describes the times of the Coronavirus Pandemic that followed my time here in India.

Fortunately, the names of the years ahead have room for optimism. As I write now in 2021 - hopefully towards the end of the pandemic - we are now and into 2022 in a 'Plava' period, which means 'that which ferries us across'. After this transition period in 2022 – 2023, the name is 'Shubhkrut', meaning 'that which created auspiciousness'. Perhaps we can look forward to much better times if the names of the years truly indicate what to expect!

Night of Shivaratri

The final pageants on the night of Shivaratri were spectacular. Hundreds of villagers and travellers from all over the world came to the ashram. Once it was dark, everyone carried lamps and lined up together to form a colossal corridor of lights that circumvented most of the ashram grounds. The sea of tiny flames shimmered in the rising heat of the darkness as we all chanted some of the holy mantras of ancient times. It was a spectacular and uplifting scene, and there was a feeling of great power, divinity and inspiration in the energies now shared between us.

Festivities continued through the night, with Sharavana entering another Bhava trance. This time he danced and was entranced as the form of Nataraj – the dancing form of Shiva. Again he sat in a trace, and the crowd listened intently to the channelled prophecies for the future.

Here in India, the classical world was still alive. What I saw reminded me of what life must have been like in ancient Greece when the Pythia priestesses of the Temple of Apollo at Delphi made their predictions. It is interesting to ponder whether our western culture had also evolved from the same roots as these Indian traditions. I had read recently that in the ruins of Delphi, they found a stone called an 'omphalos' that very closely resembles a shiva lingam. According to Greek myth, Zeus placed it after sending two eagles to each end of the universe. In the Shiva Purana, the shiva lingam is where Shiva appeared and sent Brahma (as a swan) and Vishnu (as a boar) to each end of the cosmos. Could it be that our cultures have much more in common than we thought?

Throughout the night, a choir of women chanted the Panchakshara mantra: Om Namah Shivaya. They had been chanting continually in shifts for days now, and now the mantras persisted into the night and the early hours of the morning. During the night, Sharavana gave talks and performed various poojas in the temple complex.

As the dawn broke, the final chants to Shiva were sung, and the festivities ended. We had moved from darkness to light, ignorance to knowledge.

Swami summarised what all this was about: "When you came to this earth, you were free," he said. But now you have burdens. Shiva will uplift you. It is hard to know Shiva. He will be with you always, but it is hard to know him. Externally it is easy. But internally, it is much harder. If you comprehend that you ARE Shiva, then it is easy to be uplifted. You are at Maha Shivaratri: Become Shiva! It is our job to carry the burden and illuminate the God within you."

CHAPTER 22

Pandemic and Predictions

It was clear as we made our return flights that the coronavirus was now a global problem. Most countries had not been affected at this stage, but the news said there had been new outbreaks in South Korea and Italy. As we queued for passport control, a large group of Italians passed us all wearing face masks. On the ashram, I had been away from the constant news that invades our lives. Now it was clear that the rumours about a possible pandemic were becoming a reality.

I had received several texts from my daughter Danielle warning me that she feared the virus would spread everywhere and that I should be careful. Rumours had it that Kerala had cases. The Diabetes forums and newsgroups were alight with posts, and urgent warnings of its dangers as the virus were hazardous for people with diabetes. Danielle, of course, was worried for her son Damian who you will remember has type 1 diabetes. I was leaving the strange world of India for an even stranger world ahead, a place of facemasks, social distancing and lockdowns that felt like the stuff of science fiction.

It was another challenging journey home, but this time with no delays. I arrived on our doorstep tired and unkempt, looking like a hobo. Jane was shocked, and our cat Boo dashed for the cat flap.

"You're not coming in with feet that colour!" she exclaimed, pointing to my filthy sandaled feet. I'd been walking barefoot for most of my stay at the ashram, so they were stained black from the dirt roads and now looked like black gangrened appendages. Jane reappeared with a steaming bowl of hot water and a sturdy bristled scrubbing brush.

"Scrub!" she ordered. Finally, I was allowed to step my flame-red incandescent feet onto our pristine white carpet, and then we hugged.

Jane uttered my favourite words. "I've prepared you something to eat," she said. "Plain white rice with a simple vegetarian topping. And a glass of water."

She was joking, of course. I devoured the meal, gave Jane the Saris that I had so bravely bought on the dark roads of India and then went to bed. I slept for fourteen hours.

A few days later, we both came down with flu. It was one of the worst flues that we have ever experienced, and we were both in bed for a week and had a cough for another week. We assumed that it was just a nasty cold as, at that stage, there was very little on the news about the symptoms of coronavirus.

We stayed indoors and sat it out, and made a point of not visiting anyone for over two weeks.

I have no idea whether we had the disease, but I later saw a YouTube post from an Indian man I had got to know on the ashram and said that he had caught Covid19. He explained how close he'd come to death and how Sharavana had intervened to pull him through and save his life. Perhaps the same had happened to Jane and me, and we'd contracted it, but we were lucky to get mild symptoms.

On March 23rd 2020, the UK went into lockdown. The public was told that they would only be allowed to leave their homes for limited reasons, including food shopping, exercise once per day, medical need and travelling for work when necessary. Shops selling non-essential goods had to close, gatherings of more than two people in public were banned, events including weddings - but excluding funerals - were cancelled. The nation came to a standstill.

Lockdown

Bored with TV and Netflix, many people turned to YouTube to fill the hours of boredom that accompanied lockdown. My YouTube channel started to get a lot of hits. Viewers took a particular interest in one video I had made in which I predicted that a global pandemic would hit the world. I had expected it would happen before 2020, so it wasn't 100% accurate, although many now say that the Chinese had been covering things up.

I was as shocked as everyone else by the scale of the pandemic. Although I'd made my predictions – and the national press had even taken them up in the

UK – it was nonetheless weird to be living through it. When I make predictions, they often come as if from somewhere else, as if it's not me doing all of this at all. I feel that they are given to me by the Universe, and I have very little to do with it. The consequence is that when I return to look at my predictions – particularly the ones that have happened to the letter – it is as if someone else has made them. I am just as mystified by them as people who follow my predictions online.

Now my viewers were urging me to make more predictions about the pandemic and what would happen next. I had feelings about this, but as this affected me personally, how could I be sure that my thoughts and expectations were not getting in the way of the truth. I wrote down my insights and what I felt would result from this pandemic. Perhaps the naadis would know? Maybe some of the Naadi readers I knew could give me some additional insights? If this corresponded with my clairvoyant insights, we could perhaps understand the spiritual reason for this dreadful cataclysm?

Naadi Predictions

I was able to get information from four unconnected Naadi sources and compare the results. The most important and reliable of these was Kim Paisol, one of the world's experts on the Naadi. I also spoke with Mr Prakash, who had helped me with my remedies when I made the film Mystic Journey to India and the Naadi expert Wing Commander Shasikant Oak. I also found some other Naadi readers and sources from my contacts. One of these was

Thomas Ritter in Germany, who had been taking people to India to find their Naadis for many years.

Ritter's Naadis was published in 2006 and are now available on the Internet. I noticed that it appears to predict the pandemic saying:

"After 2018, another strange disease will kill hundreds of thousands of human lives in the U.S., Europe, Asia. The infected person easily gets ill by normal diseases such as colds, as their organism cannot deal with them. Death usually arrives within three days. In most cases, the disease causes death."

Ritter points out that the Naadi reader - Ganeshbabu Sastri - called the disease by an English acronym RISC-Rapid Immune System Collapse, the accelerated collapse of the immune system. Clearly, this Naadi is right about the 'strange disease' and its similarity to the common cold, but death does not arrive within three days, nor is its mortality rate as high as suggested here.

I have a few problems with this Naadi and some of the other predictions that Ritter published, and I have not been able to authenticate the Naadi myself. This Naadi was also published in Der Spiegel, a famous German news magazine and resulted in many scepticism claims. In particular, Armin Risi, a Swiss author, said it was not genuine. With so much controversy surrounding this Naadi, I would leave this to others to battle out and return to sources I know personally.

Nonetheless, it is interesting to note that this Naadi also foresees another virus, called Kunu and caused parasite worms in the blood and civil war in the USA. Writing now, after the US elections in 2020, this possibility would have been unthinkable in 2006.

It is also something that I have predicted in my YouTube predictions made long before discovering the work of Ritter.

In my YouTube prediction, I suggested two years before the events that a pandemic would hit with a virus that had been designed in a lab. Terrorists would be blamed for the release. The Ritter Naadi appears to back up what I was saying: "It was only after decades in the period after the year 2048, will be aware that it was for RISC to a biological weapon that was released at the instigation of influential circles in the U.S. to address the population growth."

My thoughts were that the virus was released to put a halt to the riots in Hong Kong. The Chinese designed it to carry other diseases that could wipe out specific genetic types. The Covid19 was dreadful but not deadly to everyone infected. Some time into the pandemic Dr Anthony Tu at Colorado State University released a statement in Japan that they found four molecules in coronavirus that don't exist in nature. The suggestion was that coronavirus had been developed to infect people easier by artificially inserting four HIV-derived gene sequences into the genetic sequence of the SARS virus.

The Chinese were also not very helpful with information about biosecurity at the virus lab in Wuhan, China. The official explanation that it started in the Wuhan 'wet market' from bats but first passed through an intermediary animal such as a pangolin was difficult for the public to accept. My feeling is that it came from the Wuhan lab, but the Korakkar Naadi suggests otherwise, saying: "In 2020 years many countries people will die because of eating poison animals. This will affect all the people of the

World."

Before describing the Coraonavirua, the Maha Shiva Naadi talks about how during this Kali Yuga period, there will be many false gurus and leaders who will 'poison the minds of people and they will deceive and cheat the people for their own greed and selfishness.' It talks about how power and wealth are used to keep people poor and that 'people will be used as a dice game.'

It then describes the virus: "this virus, this complexity has been created by the waste and rubbish. This present situation is very similar to war; we can say this is a virus war. This is an indirect war. The war started from waste and rubbish. These kinds of conspiracies will begin to open up at some point in time in the future."

It appears that the Naadis may have different views about whether the virus was manufactured and deliberately released or an animal virus that has mutated and jumped to humans. Both the Korakkar Naadi and the Maha Shiva Naadi said that the pandemic would end by Summer 2020, but this was not the case. They all gave various mantras, homas and ayurvedic remedies that could help boost your immunity to the disease. I shared these with people on my YouTube channel.

The naadis also predicted public unrest in the wake of the pandemic. They also expect that there will be greater spirituality because of it. The Korakkar naadi says: "It will finish very soon and afterwards there will be good experiences and people will find their destiny. These will be spiritual experiences."

The Agastya Jeeva Naadi – the same one that I consulted about my grandson Damian's condition-tells us that this pandemic has been sent to push the world into a more spiritual direction:

"This is a deadly disease given by Lord Jesus, all the Rishis, the Sage of Sages, the Lord of everything and the power of the world. Let everything happen and be as ordained. It may look like a curse and appear like the effect of a crushed eclipse. It is all to crush those who do not see. Finally, Dharma will be reestablished! Surrender to Lord Shiva! Surrender.

"No one knows that Lord Shiva dances on the head of Ethan/Satan, which is happening in the name of Corona, which has come to wipe out the dirt of injustice and evil on this planet.

"This is to remind the people of the world about dharma and karma. People and the rulers of the world have forgotten how to think. All will have fear as if the world is drowning in the sea.

"In the past ages, it has been predicted that the total number of diseases related to humanity is 4448. There will be medicine for it, all of them at different times. But humanity is to forget about their karma and other deep reasons for these diseases. It is what people call human disease.

"Even though there is medicine for some of these deadly diseases, then no disease can be solved without understanding the reason why any disease comes and troubles the world. Much more of this can be read in the Kandam books by Mahaguru Agastya.

"For all diseases, medicine is already there by the grace of Jesus, Sages and God. Prayer, fire offerings and so on are beneficial too."

Into the Golden Age

I know that several other Jeeva Naadis speak about the virus and the present crisis. All of them concur that this is something temporary. All of the Jeeva naadis focus on the fact that we must learn from what is happening. Humankind must once again realize the great importance of Sathya and Dharma, i.e. truth and perfect moral and ethical behaviour.

When ignorance clouds the world and people hanker after material pleasures, the world's energy becomes heavy, and it attracts things such as viruses and diseases. These things occur to force us to shift the focus of our attention, to awaken and disperse the darkness caused by rampant materialism. This truth, says the oracles, is clear to the spiritual seeker looking for answers but unclear to those seeking answers in the mundane. It is an elementary and self-evident truth.

I am sure that there are still more troubles to come as we emerge from the age of darkness that is Kali Yuga. In the ancient Indian prophecies and, in particular, in the Puranas, a time is foreseen then the world enters a state of great moral decay. Many of these prophecies have already happened. It says that in the Kali Yuga, 'wealth alone will be the deciding factor of nobility [in place of birth, righteous behaviour or merit]. And brute force will be the only standard in establishing or deciding what is righteous or just.'

The holy texts talk of moral decay too: 'Mutual liking (and not family pedigree, social status, etc.) will be the deciding factor in choosing a marriage partner; cheating will be the order of the day in business relations; satisfaction of sexual pleasure will be the only consideration of male or female excellence and worthiness, and the wearing of the sacred thread (Yajnopavita) [and not pious behaviour or Vedic or Shastric learning] will be the outward index of being a Brahmin.'

All of the above and more is foreseen as the hallmark of the times in which we all live. The same messages are reinforced in the Ramayana, the Mahabharata and the Vishnu Purana. The great Indian philosopher Swami Vivekananda who died in 1902, also believed that we are in the midst of the move from the age of darkness to the golden age but that these times would have a prelude of difficult times.

He said: 'But greater than the present deep dismal night...no pall of darkness had ever before enveloped this holy land of ours. And compared with the depth of this fall, all previous falls appear like little hoof-marks.'

Happier Days to Come

The good news is that these difficult times will pass and herald in a new and better age – a golden age. The superhuman beings who wrote the Vedas had powers of prophecy that are unimaginable to the ordinary person. Written in these, the world's oldest scriptures, are reliable prophecies from people who had attained the highest levels of consciousness. With direct perception, reason and revealed knowledge, these ambassadors of truth could see far into our world's past, present, and future. They also wrote of the destiny of other planets and the fate of the universe itself.

The evil effects of the Age of Kali Yuga are already upon us. Many more calamities may happen in the near future, too but there is also hope on the horizon. In the Brahma-vaivarta Purana, Krishna tells Ganga Devi that there will be a Golden Age within the Kali Yuga that will begin 5,000 years after the start of Kali Yuga.

It is surmised that we are at the beginning of this Golden Age, for Krishna departed 5,000 years ago. The dawn of better times is upon us, and this period of happiness will last for 10,000 years. In these times, spiritual awareness will flourish everywhere, and a new species of humanity will evolve.

The Bhagavad Gita says that this Golden Age will see the birth of a great avatar and other holy men who will lead humankind towards these better times. It says: 'Whenever there is the decline of righteousness And rise of unrighteousness, To protect the virtuous and to destroy the wicked, I incarnate myself from age to age.' Kalki, also called Kalkin, is the prophesied tenth avatar of the Hindu God Vishnu. His birth will be the end of the Kali Yuga.

Some say that the Avatar of the new age was Sathya Sai Baba and his future incarnation as Prema Sai.

With the dawn of the new age, many other great enlightened teachers will be incarnated on the earth. We see this in people like Saharvana Baba and many others like him who will be with us soon.

With the energy shift to these better times, the old materialistic and selfish cycles will break. At this point, free will comes into play; in that, we have a choice to either let it happen by force through cataclysm, apocalypse and calamity, or we herald it in through a worldwide awakening.

People like Sharavana walk amongst us so that we choose the latter option.

CHAPTER 22

Remain Happy

On 23rd May 2020, and during the height of the pandemic, I had a strange dream about writing this book in the Prasanthi Nilayam ashram of Sathya Sai Baba in Puttaparthi. The place looked both familiar and unfamiliar at the same time. I noticed that a long wall divided the ashram. To get to either side, devotees had to enter a tall building, go up or down in an elevator until they found a floor that allowed them through to the other side. I did not know the protocol, so I walked around the side of the lift and got to the other side without using it. 'This is all nonsense,' I say. 'It's all the same level.'

I walk towards a small wooden temple. The ground beneath my feet feels spongy, and I notice that a thin layer of grass turf is laid over the landscape to disguise a massive area of slippery cow slurry. Everywhere there is sewage and the stench of effluent.

Standing pristine like a white lotus in a dirty pond, I see Sathya Sai Baba's figure dressed in white. With him is Sharavana Baba. The two figures merge to become one single figure. I find myself joking and laughing with Sathya Sai Baba and Sharavana Baba in this combined form. Their faces transfigure between the two forms and personalities. Sathya Sai Baba tells me to inform people about the correlation, and I must write about the similarities and differences.

I notice that we are now in the Sai Kulwant Hall. There are thousands of white-clad devotees, and students sat around us. Sathya Sai Baba winks at me and says, 'Watch this. They all want interviews, and this is my secret sign.'

Sathya Sai Baba then pinches his tunic, and everyone falls prostrate to the ground. 'I'm not like that,' I say. 'We are all God.'

The dream scene changes and I find myself on a hill tending cows. The cows can talk, but I struggle to understand what they are saying. The cows try and speak again but are now vomiting slurry. Amongst them is a radiant white bull that communicates with a friendly, beautiful voice. A man stands to my left. I can sense him in my peripheral vision. I cannot see him, but I know that he is my close friend. He says, 'This bull is our friend. You can even ride him if you like.'

I look again at the white bull that smiles at me like the Chesire cat from Alice in Wonderland. I am amazed at how beautiful the animal is. Its hide glows an incandescent white and is painted with red and yellow religious markings. It has a golden saddle and horns made of pure gold. The bull speaks to me: 'Have no fear for the herd that is sick. I am well. All will be well. Be Happy.'

I can hear people in the distance performing a play. I look down, and I am holding the transcript of a Shakespearean play. I see the name Cordelia.

Thank you for letting me indulge you in my dream – I'm sure Carl Jung would have had a field day with it as it is full of archetypes and unique content. It is what he would have called a 'Grand Dream,' a dream that has a mythical quality that often occurs at significant times or transitional periods in our life. They leave you with a sense of awe.

If you have read my other books, you will know that dreams about Sathya Sai Baba are momentous and do not happen by chance. They are luminous and unambiguous. Sathya Sai Baba says, 'Dreams are the reflection, reaction and resound of that which is within you. The same does not apply to the dreams in which Swami appears. Swami appears in dreams only when He wills it and not when you want.'

My Naadis have also said that the Rishis and Shiva will speak to me through my dreams. Dreams about Sathya Sai Baba are so extraordinarily lucid that it feels that you are experiencing Him in reality. I want to share this dream with you, for I believe that it is a prophecy.

The first part showing the partitioning of Puttaparthi symbolises the divisions in the Sathya Sai Baba organisation – something in which I am not involved with so able to bypass. There have been several men and women who claim to be channels for the deceased Sai Baba. Some will behave as if his invisible 'subtle form' is walking with them, and they will open car doors for his ghost and so on, and there are others who say that Sai Baba is speaking through them or that they are his sole representative here on earth. All of this is creating divisions.

In my dream, Sathya Sai Baba and Sharavana Baba are shown to be the same being. If, as we are told, you cannot dream about Sathya Sai Baba unless he wills it, then this dream must have a special significance, but I certainly do not want to add to the confusion that I have described above. What I take away from it is that the energy of Sathya Sai Baba can radiate through a few highly attuned beings. Still, they are not necessarily the awaited incarnation of the Sathya Sai Baba. I think the lady I wrote about earlier got it right when she said to me, "Sai Baba is God. Sharavana Baba is my guru."

Many that I spoke to at the ashram in Kerala had no problem with this – they agree that God's light can shine through many forms. For others, it feels like a betrayal to have more than one guru. If Sathya Sai Baba willed this dream, then maybe it can allay these fears. Of course, the way to find out is to wait until you have a dream about Sathya Sai Baba or Sharavana Baba and ask them for yourself!

This dream happened just before the gradual ending of the coronavirus lockdown, and for me, the most important message comes from the white bull. It was only after writing the dream down that meaning of a white bull became clear. The bull must be the mythical bull Nandi that is the vehicle of Shiva. The familiar figure out of sight on my left is Shiva. The stinking effluent and the puking cows are humanity beset by the Coronavirus.

Further research tells me that the Sanskrit word 'Nandi' has the meaning of happiness, joy, and satisfaction. The message is that the herd of humanity may be sick, but soon we will be well again, and happiness, joy, and satisfaction will prevail. The bull stands pristine and firm, as do the white-clad figures of Sathya Sai Baba and Sharavana Baba, who look like lotus flowers in the mud of disease and ignorance. We must have no fear for the future, says the dream. Be like Cordelia, who in Shakespeare's play about the mad King Lear was the only one who never lost faith in her father and is a symbol of the triumph of love and forgiveness over hatred and spite. Let's hope that we allow our hearts to listen to the truth and free ourselves from the hangman of ignorance.

When I told Jane about the dream as we were recording a 'psychics in lockdown' for YouTube, she reminded me of the dream she had about Sharavana and how this dream had happened some weeks before mine.

'I had a dream before yours,' says Jane 'where Sharavana came to me, and he held his right hand with two fingers down (Apana Mudra) and in his left hand, had an orange Tigerlily. Then a beautiful rainbow went all around me. He smiled and looked happy. He wore a yellow robe and said, "Be Happy. You will always be beautiful, and I will always protect you."'

Selfishness is one of the worst disorders of the modern age. Repeated acts of selfishness lead to dire consequences not only for everyone who comes into contact with the selfish person but also for the world. We are all a product of our repeated behaviour, for every time we have a selfish thought, it cuts a channel into our brain that gets deeper and deeper until selfishness becomes our default response. The result is that selfish acts create a selfish person. I have never in all my days ever seen a happy selfish person. Selfishness is one of the main reasons why so many people have become so depressed in this age of plenty.

The pandemic and all the troubles that will beset the world in the future are mainly the results of selfishness. A pandemic may have a physical cause, such as a filthy wet market of a biological experiment gone wrong, but the real reason is our lousy karma that allows things like this to become a possibility. If we can collectively reach a higher state of consciousness, then we enter a higher level of reality and the material world changes along with us. Spirit is greater than the material. Together we can make miracles happen.

In these times of corrupt politics, business and religion, we must rediscover honesty. This is something that Sharavana Baba talks about many times and is, for me, one of the main takeaways from his teachings. How many public figures today do we see as examples of integrity and truthfulness? Everywhere we see lying, cheating and theft. Few people are trustworthy, loyal, fair and sincere. Worst of all, we are not honest with ourselves.

In many ways, the pandemic – and other troubles in the world – are like the Samudra Manthan. The ocean of milk is churned, and it revealed all within that was good and evil. Out came a terrible poison that Lord Shiva swallowed to save the world, turning his throat blue. But many valuable things were also found to be shared amongst the Devas and Asuras. Finally, the ocean gave us the nectar that would make the Gods immortal—churning forces the truth out.

Donald Trump and the challenging politics of the modern age have been part of this process of transformation. Trump was a pretty weird, unusual person, that love him or hate him, was required because the USA needed a cat thrown among the pigeons. A country where too many people had been feathering their own nests for too long, looking after their own interests at the cost of destruction of the world and the poor person. We needed something wild thrown into the midst. A stir was needed, and Trump provided that – a stir that is throwing up all that was hidden before allowing America, a country that has lost its way and is in search of its soul, to settle back into a different, new order.

The troubles that may come our way, the new revolution in China, the wars over Taiwan, China's attempted invasion of India, the break up of the EU, the huge volcanic activity and floods ahead, the humbling of America and the other things I have predicted in my prophecies for the world can only happen if we let them. We do not need the poison if we chase the nectar. Our job must be to rise out of the swirling water and attain the highest spiritual level we can. If we do this, we will become happy individuals, and reality itself will undergo a metamorphosis.

We just have to keep on stirring. If we don't, then Nature will do it for us.

Seeking Happiness in Love

A good remedy for the sickness of selfishness is to give and keep on giving. It may seem that you are forever giving and get nothing back in return, but the universe recognises a kind heart's actions and will eventually reward the giver. The greatest reward is that new channels are cut into your behaviour and also into your soul. You BECOME a giving person, and the prize is happiness. When the time is right, you also start receiving, for the universe gives back a thousandfold to those who give freely from the heart.

It is the same, too, with emotions. Many people approach gurus, mediums and clairvoyants, lamenting that no one loves them and they are all alone in life. The number one question is, 'when will I met my soulmate?' They think it is something that will just come to them, but this too takes effort. If you want love in your life, you have to become a loving person. This type of action is the same law that applies when a guru steps into your life. When the student is ready, the guru will appear, they say. You do not have to seek the guru, for he will find you when you are in the right place spiritually.

In your emotional life, the same principle applies. When you are in the right inner place and act with love, then it naturally attracts love into your life. Whatever we give out comes back to us, so give out love, be loving, and love will enter your life.

Applying Spiritual Teachings

Few people know what happiness is. We confuse it with the temporary emotional satisfaction that comes with what psychologists call 'subjective well-being' – a state of pleasant emotions, moods and feelings. It's been downgraded to a brain function that is a response to our environment. Happiness comes, say the psychologists, when there is a balance of the emotions, and we have 'life satisfaction. This is what psychologists describe as when your relationships, work, achievements, and other things you consider essential are all deemed satisfactory.

But surely there is a deeper stratum to happiness? Could it be that there is a happiness that is permanent and everlasting? Even the novice seeker soon realises that the material world's happiness can only bring a temporary respite from the rigours of existence, and there must be something more profound.

The ancient Greeks thought about all of this and suggested that there are two types of happiness. The philosopher Aristotle called these: hedonia and eudaimonia. Hedonic happiness is the material happiness that comes from enjoyable experiences and sensual pleasures of the world. Eudaimonic happiness comes from seeking virtue and spiritual meaning. It is a happiness that wells from a sense of purpose and is attained by living responsibly and having others' welfare at heart. It is the happiness that dwells with us as we live a virtuous and spiritual life. In short, we can find happiness through both pleasure and meaning.

In the ancient Indian teachings, the word happiness may be translated as Sukham (pleasure) and Ananda (Bliss). In Vedanta, Gita and the Upanishads, we are told that human life's ultimate goal is not happiness but freedom. Vivekananda expressed it in a letter when he wrote, "Freedom is the goal of the universe. Nor love nor hate nor pleasure nor pain nor death nor life nor religion nor irreligion: not this, not this, not this." Gautama Buddha expressed similar ideas and told his followers that the ultimate 'happiness' is freedom from suffering.

Therefore, happiness is not the goal of existence, but it can be a path to the highest knowledge. It horrifies me that some religious people – of all faiths – are so long-faced and miserable. What has gotten into them! Spirituality should be a joy; it should be fun as the way Sahravana teaches things. Happiness is the mark of a spiritual soul or an enlightened person. We must exude the delights of existence, and all of us must stop taking ourselves, our life and our precious egos quite so seriously.

The world is a dark and terrifying place that offers us no security. If we cling to it, we find only suffering. Therefore we have to learn to tread softly over life's paths and not be sucked into the muddy way. We cannot linger; we must move on. If you stop and worry, you are deepening your delusion and creating nightmares out of your fears. Fear is not freedom.

We have the choice to be lost in delusion or to awaken to higher consciousness. As we awaken, we see that life is simply a story being told in which we are playing our part. Sathya Sai Baba expressed this clearly when he said: "Life is a game...play it. Life is a challenge; meet it. Life is a dream; realize it. Life is a sacrifice; offer it. Life is love; enjoy it."

To become free is to know that everything is God and God alone. It is the process of the Universe moving from being to becoming. From the transcendental viewpoint, we see the world and ourselves differently. We don't have to try and be spiritual, for everything is spiritual. Where once we may have seen the writhing mass of humanity as ignorant maggots, now we see them all as lotus buds flowering. In every face, we see the shining countenance of enlightened beings. The potential for happiness is everywhere.

I am not suggesting that we become aloof from life or not engage with the world. We must see happiness for what it is and understand that it comes in different forms. What we need is quality happiness that is sustainable.

Much of what is peddled as happiness remedies on Facebook and the like is a false path. Gurdjieff, an enigmatic spiritual teacher who died in 1949, had said that everyone is a spiritual idiot of one kind or another. His list included the "compassionate idiot," – a title that perfectly suits the Facebook gurus we see today. Too many seek ways to find instant happiness and quick routes that require no work or effort. A wise and intelligent person realizes that happiness is not something you are owed or given on a golden platter. Happiness has to be earned through spiritual practice that removes the veil of ignorance obscuring the joy of your true nature.

Forms of Happiness

In Indian Samkhya philosophy, they talk about three qualities called Gunas. Everything in the universe arises from the original or primary substance called Prakriti. From this ethereal Prakriti arise the three primary gunas. These are tamas (darkness, ignorance, inertia, laziness), rajas (passion, activity, movement), and sattva (light, goodness, calmness, harmonious). These qualities are present in our behaviour, thoughts, actions, food, yoga asanas, and medicine. Our nature is a mixture of all three gunas.

From this idea of the gunas, there arise three types of happiness. The first of these is Tamasic happiness which is sluggish and delusional. Examples of this sort of happiness would be getting pleasure from enjoying the misfortune of others, sarcasm, gossiping, insults, stealing, revenge, harming others and so on. You get the picture. Tamasic happiness arises from ignorance, and it is a painful and destructive form of joy. Few would admit, even to themselves, that they harbour these secret pleasures, and clearly, no spiritual awakening can come from these selfish motives.

The need for Tamasic Happiness may arise from tragedy in a person's life or a series of soul-crushing events. But to slip into a pit of envy and destructive joy is not the answer. The person may become jealous of other people's happiness or unconsciously take pleasure in seeing others fail. This behaviour is self-destructive. There is no need to de-friend the world. Tamasic Happiness must be let go of. Accept your fate and move on to better times. The stormy clouds of negative karma have cleared; now, energetically, seek something better.

The second form of happiness is Rajistic Happiness. The Bhagavad Gita (18:38) describes this earthly form of happiness as "contact between the senses and their objects, and is at first like nectar, but at last like poison." This stanza describes the commonplace form of happiness that most people seek in the external world. It can include all forms of sensual enjoyment such as over-eating, sexual activity, excessive stimulation of the senses such as loud music or visual overload, preoccupation with career, money, fame, etc. None of this is bad per-say, but the Bhagavad Gita warns us that they are temporary pleasures and dependent on the external world.

A person trapped in a cycle of Rajistic Happiness will be forever seeking insatiable pleasures, have an agitated mind, and may get swept away by the play of senses. Without moderation, it is poisonous honey. The good news is that happiness does not depend entirely on external conditions. If we develop the right inner conditions and a positive mental attitude, we can move beyond our dependency on the world to find lasting happiness.

I'm not saying that we need to put stones in our shoes and undergo austerities. The pleasures of the world are not to be rejected or natural drives repressed, but it is necessary to see beyond worldly pleasures. Enjoy the pleasures of life but have non-attachment to them. They pass and are lovely for a while, but we also need to seek self-sustaining and permanent happiness.

The highest form of happiness is Sattvic Happiness. The Bhagavad Gita (18:37) describes this as the reverse of Rajistic Happiness in that it is "at first is like poison, but at last like nectar – this kind of happiness, arising from the serenity of one's own mind, is called sattvic". This form of happiness arises with moderation and self-control, and from these qualities stems grace, contentment and self-knowledge.

The peace and joy that comes from being centred on the inner divinity give foundation to your happiness. We no longer depend on the world to find happiness. This attitude is the closest we may come to 'being happy' rather than forever 'seeking happiness'.

Sattvic Happiness may sometimes seem like an unattainable goal, but we must never give up hope of being happy. We need to remember that our innermost spirit is divine, and its essence is happiness itself. The conditions of the world are neither good nor bad; they are neutral. It is our attitude towards them that determines whether we suffer or not. Working to change our thoughts and finding inner mastery is the sure-fire way to a happier path. This path takes some discipline, but it also takes gentleness, trust in yourself, and self-education to seek higher goals. We don't want to become life-denying uptight control freaks and enemies of desire, but we do want to see beyond the shallow forms of happiness. We are fools if we forever chase a mirage.

The universe wants us to become awake – to become enlightened beings. The whole of Creation supports this goal, so we should put our spiritual goals first. We must aim high. With every step, we make towards awakening the Universe, or God, or consciousness or whatever you want to call it, will support our efforts. The world around us will change, and happiness will flower everywhere we look.

To secure happiness on earth, we need to embrace our material and spiritual needs by pursuing morality, prosperity, enjoyment, and spirituality. The ultimate happiness is found in liberation. For some, this may come early in life, but for most, the need for spiritual freedom comes once the world's obligations are fulfilled. At the end of the journey, we yearn to enter the world of bliss.

We all embody all of the above types of happiness, but to attain the highest form of happiness, we must transcend all three gunas. Dive through joy to find what lies beyond joy, and you will discover transcendental happiness. Beyond physical, mental and spiritual happiness, it is the bliss that hides behind the perceptions, behind the sense of 'me' and transcends karma.

God is everywhere, and the bliss of happiness is the foundation of His Creation. It is easy to find, for we are it. We are God. Indeed happiness is our innermost nature. You don't have to try to be happy: all we have to do is be what we already are. Be Happy!

Om Sharavanabhava

Talks and Sayings by Sharavana baba

The Power of the Gayathri Mantra

We need the blessing of our ancestors, the guru and the clan deities to enjoy life. Even enjoying our earnings requires the grace of the god.

By chanting the Gayathri Mantra with care we get the blessings of our ancestors and guru. The Gayathri mantra elevates us. It helps us to attain a position and to maintain it. The Gayathri mantra gives physical and mental strength and removes the karmas from our previous birth. It gives us a blissful life.

We must pray to the goddess Gayathri in the same way we do to Lord Agni (Fire). Agni purifies the atmosphere. In the same way it removes all impurities and enhances our inner beauty.

For whatever is important to our lives, we must embrace these ideas. For example, if we need to run we must first know the path. God Shows us the path, and the Guru lays the road. Therefore hold on to the guru and seek God.

No one can seek the guru. The guru will seek you at the right time. This is determined by the good deeds done in our previous birth.

Finding the Auspicious State

Today is an auspicious day. In Kerala, it is the day when people pay homage to Lord Krishna. We place his image amongst fruits and gold coins to represent good fortune and wealth. By doing this we bring the auspiciousness of Lord Krishna into our lives.

I wish you all an auspicious and pleasant day. What do we mean by the word auspicious? In the Tamil language, 'auspicious' translates as Mangalam which originally comes from the holy language of Sanskrit. Auspiciousness is the essence of everything; it is the supreme soul and is another name for Lord Easwara. (Lord Shiva.)

We must all find this auspicious state but how can we do this? We must first look to everything that is fortunate and auspicious in our own lives and embrace it.

Today is an auspicious day because of the blessings from our ancestors. When we make an effort, we must have the previous efforts of our ancestors in the forefront of our thoughts. This will draw upon the power of auspiciousness and make us successful. Life is a struggle, but without struggle, there is no success. The salt is in the seawater, but without effort, we cannot harvest it.

The guru will help us in our efforts, for he shows us the light and the path. He provides us with whatever is necessary at the appropriate time. All have to do the same: we have to lead our life in light and guide others. We need to seek the foot of the guru for salvation. This is achieved through chanting and constant thoughts of God."

Adma Seva, Mantra Seva and Karma Seva

We must be dedicated to the cause. Only then will we get what we want. God gave us this life and world. Some aspects we can see, others not. For that, we need the divine light to find it.

From prayers we will attain inner brightness. This will lead us to prasadam (divine food/mercy) and, through this, we acquire Punya (divine reward for good deeds).

We must accumulate an abundance of this. There is no need to accumulate wealth more than necessary. Punya will protect our clan, family and the society. To get Punya, we need to claim the mountain with sincere devotion.

In this Age of Kali Yuga we must do the following service:

Adma Seva. This is Dhyana (Meditation) to realize

the inner self.

Mantra Seva This is Japa (Chanting) which brings progress in life.

Karma Seva –These are the pooja (rituals) to attain salvation.

We must be complete in the above. This will lead us to salvation.

The Mrityunjaya mantra will help us to conquer death. The word 'death' is not only relevant to the body, but we also need to protect our family and the society from death.

We must take appropriate measures to remove the suffering of others. Constant spiritual practice is a must. If we take a stone and keep it in our hand, nothing will happen, but if we make an effort and sculpt it, it will become a deity.

Like a child in the womb, we must perform Adma sadhana (Spiritual Practice). We must close our worldly eyes and open the inner eyes. This is known as meditation. This will elevate us. Through this we will see God as the light within us.

Lord Hanuman always chanted the name of Lord Rama. Constant chanting will make us speak adequately, sweetly and pleasantly. This will make us very likeable and eliminate any misunderstanding.

If you want to visit Lord Ayyappa (the Hindu god of growth) during the festival time, you need to take Irumudi (offerings). This is karma yoga.

From the river banks of Pampi, we can only see the Lord Ganesh temple. To see the Ayyappa we need to claim 18 steps. We must be in complete service.

Lord Arjuna was very close to lord Krisha in Gurusesthira war, like that we are facing many challenges today. Therefore we also need to embrace god with adma seva, mantra seva and karma seva.

Mrityunjaya Mantra

Om tryambakam yajamahe sugandhim pustivardhanam urva rukamiv bandhanan mrtyor muksiya mamrtat

Translation: We worship Lord Shiva (three eyed), who is our nurturer. We pray him to give us liberty from confinements of death just as a cucumber gets plucked very easily from its roots.

Some Quotations

Nothing is impossible if we are grounded in wisdom.

Learn to see God in everything, even in a firefly.

One needs to be very soulful, have time on hand and have patience. Only then we can realize our true selves and achieve success in life. Even if either of them is missing, it won't lead to proper results. Then you must have self-belief and courage.

Sri Krishna is your soul; Sri Radha is your body. They should not hurt each other in any manner. They should be in consonance. Focus on Sri Krishna (Your soul) and perform your Sadhana while staying rooted with Sri Radha (your body) to win over the situations in life.

Tame your wandering mind through Dhyana (Meditation), Japa (Chanting) and Pooja (Worship).

Strive to overcome the gunas.

You enter a temple only to see your Self.

Even if you cannot instruct, try and obey what is instructed.

Know that there is an energy behind all your actions.

Embrace that which enhances goodness, not evil.

If a son hurts his mother, he runs the risk of her complaints and possibly leaving him. This is the worst sin. The son will have to undergo even more pain than the mother in due course of time.

If you want others to pray for you, first you must pray for them.

Do not blame others, for there are faults hidden even in the best of us.

Do not immerse yourself in the whirlpool of life.

Perceive both the haves and have-nots with equal vision.

Convert your actions into offerings.

If you work hard, all the joys that you lost can be retrieved.

Never forget Me in your actions, even if you lack comforts.

God is where luxuries are discarded.

You have come not to see Me but to serve Me.

The light inside you lies in erasing the pain in others.

When you are in the presence of a Sadhguru, silence is the best language.

Time will not give us opportunities always. But when time gives us opportunities, you must seize it and make the best of it.

Lengthen your day and spend more time in service to others. Cut down the sleep time, as you have come here to serve others and realize yourself.

Prepare for tomorrow, but live your life completely today.

Any aspect of God is attainable through the chanting of mantras, holy verses or sacred names of God.

The sugarcane looks like a piece of rod. But when you take it and squeeze the cane, you will get sweet juice. Similarly, you have to make that effort to derive the benefits of the guru.

You can't contain the sunlight in your palm, but sunlight is all around you. You are in that light. That is divine. Tap into that source and experience the divine.

Embrace that which gives you consciousness, not that which causes you to become unconscious.

Perform all actions after taking permission from the four pillars, including Father, Mother, Guru and God.

Exercise caution when travelling on the path of life by having the wisdom to remain unattached to its pleasures.

Do not expect a guru to clear all your problems. Instead, pray for wisdom and strength to face challenges and overcome them with courage.

God can be made to appear by the chanting of mantras, and the power of divine energy can also be experienced.

No mistake is committed in ignorance. They are invariably committed with awareness.

If you need something, you have to go in search of it. It is your responsibility to search, but it is God's will to give.

Be Strict, Be Strong and Be Straight. Only in this manner you shall receive the courage to face any challenge in life and be victorious.

MORE INFORMATION:

omsharavanabhavamatham.org.uk

MESSAGES FROM THE UNIVERSE
By Craig Hamilton-Parker
ISBN 978-1517568887

Read the incredible story of Craig's encounter with the Naadi Oracle of India and how it predicts the future with 100% accuracy – including the future day of his death. Craig tells the story of his encounter with the oracle and writes about the implications of fate and destiny.

The book also tells of Craig and his wife Jane's work as a mediumistic couple and how they travel the world, giving readings to celebrities and meeting holy people as they fulfil the startling predictions made by the oracle.

This book is the prequel to *'Mystic Journey to India'* and tells the mind-boggling predictions that take Craig to India to do the magic remedies.

MYSTIC JOURNEY TO INDIA
(FILM AND BOOK)
by Craig Hamilton-Parker
ISBN 978-1974280872

Inspired by the startling predictions made by the Naadi Oracle, Craig embarks on a journey to India to fulfil the oracle's prophecies and clear his karma. He meets the Naadi readers, and together they travel to remote parts of India to do rituals and meet holy men.

On the journey, they meet a Siddha yogi who can sleep in a raging fire and has incredible things to tell the spiritual seekers. *Mystic Journey to India* is available as a **book** and also as a **film**. You can watch the movie on Amazon Prime.

WHAT TO DO WHEN YOU ARE DEAD
by Craig Hamilton-Parker
ISBN 978-1508521754

What to Do When You Are Dead is a landmark book" – Psychic News

Is there life after death? In this book, Craig draws on cross-cultural beliefs and his work to describe what life is like in the afterlife. This book will help you to overcome the fear of death and prepare you for the next life.

Based on extensive research and direct insights, the book builds a picture of the afterlife and what life is like on the other side.

All Books are available from Amazon or at the author's website psychics.co.uk

ABOUT THE AUTHOR

Craig Hamilton-Parker is a British author, television personality and professional psychic medium. He is best known for his TV shows *Our Psychic Family, The Spirit of Diana, Nightmares Decoded* and *Mystic Journey to India.*

On television, he usually works with his wife Jane Hamilton-Parker, who is also a psychic medium. Their work was showcased in a three-part documentary on the BBC called *Mediums Talking to the Dead.*

Craig and Jane have a not-for-profit foundation that helps the poor in India and has the long-term ambition to build a spiritual centre.

Find out more about Craig & Jane's work, lectures and public appearances:

Craig & Jane Hamilton-Parker website:
psychics.co.uk

Foundation website:
hamiltonparker.org

Printed in Great Britain
by Amazon